THE SOUTH DOWNS WAY

by
Kev Reynolds

2 POLICE SQUARE, MILNTHORPE, CUMBRIA LA7 7PY
www.cicerone.co.uk

Printed by KHL Printing, Singapore.
A catalogue record for this book is available from the British Library.
All photographs are by the author.

This book is for Charlie Moon

Updates to this Guide

While every effort is made by our authors to ensure the accuracy of guidebooks as they go to print, changes can occur during the lifetime of an edition. If we know of any, there will be an Updates tab on this book's page on the Cicerone website (www.cicerone.co.uk), so please check before planning your trip. We also advise that you check information about such things as transport, accommodation and shops locally. Even rights of way can be altered over time. We are always grateful for information about any discrepancies between a guidebook and the facts on the ground, sent by email to info@cicerone.co.uk or by post to Cicerone, 2 Police Square, Milnthorpe LA7 7PY, United Kingdom.

Front cover: Cuckmere Haven is a great vantage point from which to study the Seven Sisters

CONTENTS

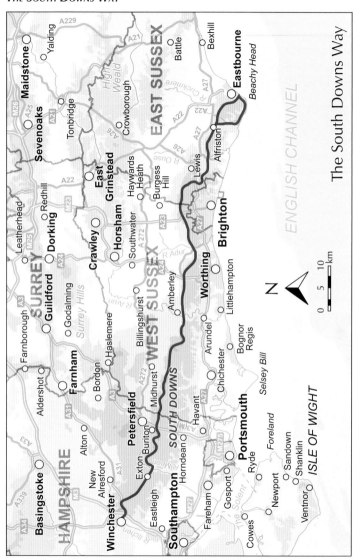

INTRODUCTION

The start to a bright spring day... striding through a gentle downland valley with the delightful name of Cricketing Bottom, settling into that easy comfortable rhythm so essential to the full enjoyment of a long walk. The early sun warm overhead, my first cuckoo of the year calling from the hillside, the smoky haze of bluebells lining scrub-crowded slopes where the blackthorn produces haloes of flower. Only the pheasants complain. Larks rise singing, and all around swell the Downs. Within less than an hour I'll be on their crest. Within that hour I'll be wandering alone save for the peewits and skylarks and hares, save for the cowslips at my feet and the orchids in the spinneys. Alone with the faintest of breezes and huge views that have the sea gleaming in one direction, and the vast tartan plain of the Weald in the other. Hour upon hour wandering through history, past burial mounds and hill forts left by the first wanderers of this Way, on land that once was covered by sea but is now serenaded day by day by minute specks of birds whose land this really is, on grasslands grazed by slow-moving fluffs of sheep, the close-cropped hillsides darkened now and then by the sweeping shadows of clouds. Cloud-shadows – the only impatience on the South Downs Way.

Jevington, midway between Eastbourne and Alfriston

More than a decade has passed since I first walked the South Downs Way, but I have been back several times, drawn by the visual delights to be won from the crest of this southern backbone of land with its overwhelming sense of space and peace, whose trails seem to wind on for ever – towards a dim, blue, never-to-be-reached, horizon. And each time I tread that smooth baize of turf and look north across the empty Weald, I find it hard to believe that this is the 'overcrowded' South of England.

This South is a surprisingly secret land, though its secrets are there to be unravelled if one only cares to look. It is misjudged and often maligned, and walking through and across it is the only way properly to discover its truths, for by wandering these ancient footpaths one absorbs its essence through the soles of the feet. The cyclist and horse rider will also develop an affinity with the land, but without the direct physical contact known by the walker, a unique part of the experience will be missing.

Along the South Downs Way your field of vision expands with the miles to a greater knowledge of the land. The traveller begins to appreciate that it is not so populous as is generally thought, that its countryside is infinitely more varied than might previously have been considered possible of the lowlands, and when you gain the scarp edge it is the panoramic expanse which throws into disarray any preconceived notion that mountains have a monopoly of landscape grandeur. Here the perspective fits. Scale is adjusted and beauty comes

Celandines bank the trails with gold in April and May

The view from Firle Beacon

from order. In a world of constant change there is something reassuring in a vast acreage of countryside that somehow survives without too many scars – another eye-opener for the rambler in the South.

There are other surprises too, but these must be left for the wanderer, cyclist and horse rider to discover for him or herself, for along the South Downs Way any journey is bound to be full of rewards. Journeys of delight, journeys of discovery.

None but the walker can possibly understand the full extent of that statement, for it is only by the slowing of pace that one finds the ability to become part of the landscape itself. This is not something that may be achieved from the seat of a motor vehicle, for motoring divorces you from the land, and at a speed which

blurs and distorts. Along country footpaths, however, there is so much to experience – from the succession of soil types beneath your feet to the nuance of every breeze that plays sculptor to the passing clouds. One breathes the fragrance of wayside plants, discovers the life of hedgerow and woodland shaw, and drifts through an unfolding series of panoramas. With senses finely tuned to the world about you, a footpath becomes a highway of constant discovery, of constant delight.

THE DOWNS

In the distant mists of time, during what is known as the Cretaceous period – that is, from about 100 million to 70 million years ago – the land we now know as the Weald lay

9

The quintessential South Downs – on Hyden Hill above the Meon Valley

beneath the waters of a warm, shallow sea whose bed was covered by a sandwich of sedimentary deposits. Miniscule shell-bearing organisms settled on this bed, the pure calcium carbonate of their shells powdering to a chalk dust that built with staggering patience to a depth of just one foot every 30,000 years or so. (Consider the time-scale required to produce the chalk cliffs of Beachy Head – over 500 feet/150m deep!) Yet this layer of soft crumbling chalk, composed of all these tiny shells, stretched from the Thames Valley to the Pas de Calais, and reached a depth of around 1000feet/300m, while into this white cheese-like rock there also settled the skeletons of sea sponges to form hard seams of flint.

Then, about 20 million years ago during the Tertiary period, came the continental collision which built the Alps. Italy was thrust into Europe and Spain was pressured from the south.

Mountains were slowly buckled and, as with a stone tossed into a pond, ripples spread in all directions. The chalk of southern England was raised into a huge dome rising from the sea and stretching for about 125 miles (200km), end to end. Weathering followed – a process that continues to this day. Rain, ice, frost, all combined to nibble away at this dome, aided and abetted by rivers and streams that found a weakness when the chalk cracked as it buckled. The outer edges of the dome were the last to crumble, the central core being carried away in watercourses that flowed through it. The centre of that lost dome is now the Weald, the outer edges the North and South Downs.

Rivers and streams continue to drain the Weald, breaching the Downs in valleys far broader than they now require, while dry knuckle coombs within the heart of this downland tell of streams that no longer exist.

Rambling along the smoothly rounded South Downs today we may wonder at this triumph of geological history. Gazing from the clifftop at Beachy Head we see the body of the land exposed, carved through as though with a gigantic scalpel. We gaze into the heart of unfathomable time, at the crushed, bleached remnants of creatures whose sacrifice is our gain.

East of the coastline, as the route of the South Downs Way leads away from the sea, that sacrifice is forgotten as we amble across grasslands rich in wild flowers. Yet beneath our boots the chalk lies deep, waiting only for the plough to expose its weaknesses to the wind. Where the path leads through arable land we see polished flints littering the fields, the chalk cushion around them turning to dust under the influence of sun and wind, ready to be brushed away. The heights of the Downs shrink in the summer breeze – one more act of sacrifice by creatures that long ago gave their shells to the southern landscape.

The common perception of the South Downs is one of rolling, flower-dazzled grasslands trimmed by sheep. This is partly due to the influence of our neolithic ancestors who crossed from continental Europe some 5000 years ago and settled here, raising animals, clearing trees and growing crops. Until their arrival the hills would have been forested, but they, and the Iron Age settlers who arrived more than 2500 years later, cleared the forests for both agricultural purposes and for fuel, creating the open spaces that are such a feature of the eastern and central Downs today. The Romans too farmed the downland for corn,

Drifts of wood anemones carpet both woodland and shaw.

and grazed their animals on the rich meadows, but following the arrival of the Normans there was a growth in the population of villages and towns snuggling at the foot of the hills, and the number and size of flocks of downland sheep grew as a consequence. From the 14th century on the area was very heavily grazed, reaching a peak 500 years later when the eastern Sussex Downs alone supported more than 200,000 ewes and lambs.

With the Second World War the nature of downland began to change once more, and in the aftermath of hostilities vast acreages were turned by the plough for the production of grain. Today the wanderer will experience a mixture of pasture, arable and woodland, a contrast that consists of meadows dancing with cowslips and the sharp golden dazzle of oil-seed rape, of yellow-headed wheat in summer and the lush foliage of beech and birchwood, of blackthorn scrub and blotches of gorse. Yet from a distance, from the low-lying Weald, the view is as Margaret Fairless Dawson (writing under the pseudonym of Michael Fairless) described it in *The Roadmender*: 'lean grey downs, keeping watch and ward between the country and the sea'.

THE SOUTH DOWNS WAY

Remaining within the South Downs National Park for almost its entire length, the official South Downs Way leads for 100 miles (160km) between Eastbourne and Winchester, following the northern escarpment for much of the way and rarely descending to habitation except where river valleys interrupt the regular course of the Downs. Opened in 1972, the South Downs Way originally finished in Buriton, near the Sussex–Hampshire border, but by the end of 1987 proposals for an extension to Winchester had been approved by the Secretary of State for the Environment.

The South Downs Way was the first National Trail to be developed as a bridleway throughout its entire length. In a few places the bridleway and footpath routes diverge but, apart from the initial (eastern) stage between Eastbourne and Alfriston, these are temporary alternatives only, and by far the majority of the Way is shared by ramblers, horse riders and cyclists.

For the greater part of its length the Way follows the northern crest of the South Downs escarpment, with broad views overlooking low Wealden farmlands as well as the rolling Downs. Nestling between downland hills to the south are the clefts of dry valleys, called 'bottoms', or 'deans'. Beyond them in the eastern sector sparkles the English Channel, but further west the nature of the landscape changes and there is less a sense of height and space, and the sea is all but a memory.

Five rivers (in Sussex these are the Cuckmere, Ouse, Adur and Arun,

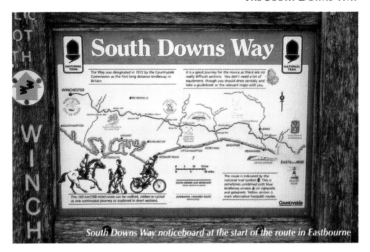

South Downs Way noticeboard at the start of the route in Eastbourne

with the lovely Meon in Hampshire) have cut valleys through the chalk, and the South Downs Way descends into – and climbs out of – them with fairly steep paths or tracks. Mostly though the route remains along the crest, sometimes on clear trackways, sometimes on flint paths, sometimes on the soft luxury of turf, and for a good part of the way it remains more than 650 feet (200m) above sea level. In the eastern half the Downs are open and exposed, but towards Hampshire woodlands become more frequent. Throughout, the quality of the route is first rate, with paths and gates well maintained and waymarking almost everywhere superb.

History is an ever-present companion to the route, for as we have seen, the crests of the Downs were long ago used by nomadic tribes as convenient highways above the dense forests and mire of the Weald. Neolithic man began to cultivate them and to mine for the flint from which he made tools. In the Bronze and Iron Ages primitive farm sites, long barrows and hill forts began to pepper the ridges, and their tell-tale signs are there to this day – although modern farm practices have destroyed evidence of a number of these in recent years. Along the route of the South Downs Way there are something like 400 Bronze Age burial barrows. There are lynchets (ancient field systems) dating from the Iron Age, rippling grass slopes where ploughed land long ago slipped against the original small field boundaries of piled stone. At Butser Hill, south of Petersfield, an Iron Age site reveals three defensive dykes, lynchets, burial mounds and ancient trackways.

The South Downs Way easing through Queen Elizabeth Forest

During the Roman occupation routes of trade and communication were engineered across the South Downs, and so advanced were their methods of construction that some of these have been adopted as modern rights of way. In places the long-distance walker uses tracks that were laid in the first century BC, and west of Bignor Hill the South Downs Way comes to a large wooden signpost bearing directions to Noviomagus (Chichester) and Londinium (London) on the line of the Roman Stane Street built around AD 70. (Half an hour's walk away are the remains of Bignor Roman Villa, while nearer to the Way are the earthworks of a Stone Age causewayed camp.)

In valley settlements Saxon and Norman churches make a brief visit worthwhile. Along the airy crestline the trail passes numerous dew ponds created one or two hundred years ago as watering holes for the huge flocks of sheep that helped give the Downs their unique character so admired today. History, then, is all around you when you journey along the South Downs Way.

Which way to walk? West to east, or east to west? There are plenty of good reasons for arguing both directions, so for this edition, the route is first described from east to west with Winchester the goal as though on a pilgrimage, then the second half of the book gives the walk in the opposite direction, starting at Winchester and ending in Eastbourne.

The westbound route begins near Beachy Head on Eastbourne's western fringe. There is an initial divergence of ways, for the bridle-way heads inland via Jevington while the main footpath route goes along the clifftop of the Seven Sisters as far as Cuckmere Haven, then north on the east bank of the river valley via Westdean and Litlington to Alfriston, where it joins the bridleway.

From Alfriston the South Downs Way climbs to Bostal Hill where paragliders sail the summer skies, then continues on to Firle Beacon, Beddingham Hill and Iford Hill before descending from the escarpment to cross a valley cut by the River Ouse at Southease. On then to Mill Hill and Swanborough Hill, across the A27 west of Lewes, then up to Balmer Down where broad views are gained across the Weald. Ditchling Beacon is invariably busy with day trippers, the twin Clayton windmills are landmarks of genuine appeal, but beyond them there's a dip to Pyecombe on the way to the Devil's Dyke. The Way continues, keeping high to cross a series of hills and, after passing the last of these (Truleigh Hill, with its youth hostel conveniently set beside the trail), the route loses much height in order to cross the River Adur at Botolphs below Steyning.

West of the Adur, Chanctonbury Ring is the major landmark, an historic circle of beech trees on an Iron Age site. Many of the trees were badly damaged by the storm which hit southern England on 16 October 1987. To the south, off the route but in view, is Cissbury Ring – one of the largest of all Iron Age hill fort sites. Washington lies

below, alongside the busy A24, but heading west the peace of the Downs is quickly regained over Kithurst Hill, Springhead Hill and Rackham Hill, from the last of which the windings of the River Arun can be seen draining the country beyond Amberley.

A new route has been created near Amberley and, where it crosses the A29 by Coombe Wood, the South Downs Way meets its midway point, marked by a signpost. The Downs now become more heavily treed and a long stretch of broad-leaved woodland accompanies the Way over Cocking Down. Pen Hill, Beacon Hill and Harting Down restore more open views, then a short woodland stretch opens along the trackway of Forty Acre Lane between South Harting and Buriton where Sussex eases into Hampshire.

Once Buriton marked the end of the walk, but it now lies a little north of the route, while the South Downs Way passes through the expanse of Queen Elizabeth Forest, where there is a possibility of sighting deer. Immediately after leaving this you climb to Butser Hill for an easy section with a far-reaching aspect.

More downland tracks lead to historic Old Winchester Hill, now a National Nature Reserve on the site of an Iron Age hill fort, where the cyclist's and horserider's bridleway diverts from the walker's route on the way to Exton. Beacon Hill is next, from where farm tracks and bridlepaths carry the Way on its final stage across Gander Down, Cheesefoot Head and

Beacon Hill can be seen across the valley from the slopes of Old Winchester Hill

Telegraph Hill, then into the small village of Chilcomb which is just one long field away from Winchester.

ACCOMMODATION

Although it is feasible to walk the South Downs Way in dislocated day-stages with the aid of private and/or public transport, this guide has been written primarily with the needs of the long-distance walker in mind. Accommodation along the way is therefore a prime concern.

Numerous options exist along or close to the route, including hotels, B&Bs, guest houses, youth hostels, camping barns and campsites, up-to-date details of which are available via the SDW website – www.nationaltrail.co.uk/south-downs-way. Booking in advance is essential because of the popularity of the region in general and the SDW in

particular, and as prices vary considerably, do check when making your reservation.

At the time of writing, there are five youth hostels conveniently sited near the South Downs Way (www.yha.org.uk). These are at Eastbourne, Alfriston, Itford Farm near Southease, Telscombe and Truleigh Hill. In addition the National Trust has a camping barn known as Gumber Bothy near Bignor Hill, which offers dormitory accommodation and camping, and there's an independent hostel, Wetherdown Lodge, which is part of a Sustainability Centre located on the Way near East Meon (www.sustainability-centre.org).

A few campsites will be found close to, or within a mile or two of, the route, and these are listed on the national trail website mentioned above. Wild camping along the South Downs Way is not really an option.

PRACTICAL ADVICE

One of the benefits to the walker of the South Downs Way being end-to-end bridleway is that for the vast majority of the route there are no stiles to contend with. It is only where the walker's route diverts from the bridleway that this traditionally English countryside obstacle has to be faced. Elsewhere, easy-to-open bridle gates make no demands on weary legs towards the end of a long day's walking. (If I ever make a fortune I'll replace every stile in southern England with a kissing gate!)

For the most part waymarking is exemplary (waymarks bear the white acorn symbol which indicates a National Trail), there are one or two places where these are rather sparse but close attention to guidebook descriptions and/or reasonable map-reading skills, will prevent you from getting lost.

The route passes through one of the driest and warmest parts of the country, and for the most part bridle-paths will be firm underfoot, but following rain the bare chalk tracks soon become very slippery, which can cause problems on steep descents. Under 'normal' summer conditions there will be little mud, while exposed flints will prove uncomfortable unless you are well shod. For long periods the traveller along the South Downs Way will be fully exposed to the elements with neither shelter nor shade for several miles. This can create problems in summer as in winter – bright sunshine can be as debilitating on a long walk as cold winds and rain. Be prepared for all eventualities.

If this is your first visit to the South Downs you will be surprised at the scarcity of villages or towns along the route – this is one of the delights, but it can also be seen as a problem.

Eastbourne Youth Hostel is conveniently situated a short distance from the SDW bridleway route

There are occasional country pubs for refreshment, but remarkably few shops. Fortunately the Society of Sussex Downsmen, in conjunction with the Countryside Agency and local authorities, has been instrumental in providing a number of drinking-water taps for walkers and riders along the Way. But all who tackle the route, whether on foot, bike or horse, are advised to fill their drinking bottles at the start of each day, and to carry food.

WALKING COMPANIES AND BAGGAGE TRANSFERS

Several companies organise guided and/or self-guided holidays on the South Downs Way, or simply book accommodation on your behalf and transfer your baggage stage by stage along the route. The following list is merely a sample, and is not comprehensive, nor should the inclusion of any company be considered an endorsement of their services.

- Contours Walking Holidays (www.contours.co.uk): self-guided; accommodation and baggage transfer; 6–10 walking days; eastbound
- Footprints of Sussex (www.footprintsofsussex.co.uk): self-guided; accommodation and baggage transfer; 7–10 nights; westbound and eastbound
- HF Holidays (www.hfholidays.co.uk): 10 walking days and 1 rest day; guided; accommodation and baggage transfer; eastbound
- Let's Go Walking (www.southdownswaywalking.com): 8 walking days; self-guided; accommodation and baggage transfer; eastbound
- Macs Adventure (www.macsadventure.com): 6–8 walking days; self-guided; accommodation and baggage transfer; eastbound
- Ramblers Holidays/Load Off Your Back (www.ramblersholidays.co.uk): 4, 5, 8 or 10 days; self-guided; accommodation; baggage transfer; eastbound
- Sherpa Expeditions (www.sherpa-walking-holidays.co.uk): 6 or 10 days; self-guided; accommodation and baggage transfer; westbound

As a National Trail the South Downs Way is well signed and waymarked

Crossing Hyden Hill the route follows an easy tree-lined track

GETTING THERE – AND BACK

Eastbourne and Winchester have good rail connections with London. Eastbourne services come from London Victoria, while those for Winchester use Waterloo. Elsewhere the South Downs Way is accessible by train with stations at Polegate, Glynde, Lewes, Hassocks and Southease. Amberley also has a station close to the route on the line to Arundel, while Petersfield, north of Buriton, has a line from London's Waterloo. Telephone numbers for railway timetable information are given in Appendix B.

For bus services and operators, download the South Downs Public Transport Guide from the website www.southdowns.gov.uk or contact Traveline on 0871 200 2233.

USING THE GUIDE

For the majority of the route waymarks and signposts are sufficient to make detailed guidebook descriptions superfluous. But in case doubts arise, or in the event of an occasional sign being vandalised or missing, the route is described as found on my most recent walking of it. That said, improvements are occasionally made to the Way which entail rerouting, and in such cases where waymarking differs from the description in this guide, you are advised to follow the waymarked alternative.

Notification of any major changes along the Way will be borne in mind for future editions of this book. A postcard detailing these, sent to me via the publisher, will be gratefully received and will be added to the Updates tab for this book on the Cicerone website.

Maps used in this guide are taken from the Ordnance Survey Landranger series at a scale of 1:50,000 (1¼ inches to 1 mile). While they show the route of each stage of the South Downs Way, walkers are recommended to consult the sheets from which they are taken to gain a wider picture of the landscape, and to locate overnight accommodation which may not appear on the limited map samples published here. Four Landranger maps cover the length of the SDW, but for greater detail the six sheets of the Explorer series at 1:25,000 (2½ inches to 1 mile) may be preferred. Details of specific map sheets are given at the heading to each stage of the walk described.

Perhaps the most convenient mapping of the South Downs Way is the doubled-sided single sheet published by Harvey at a scale of 1:40,000 (a little over 1½ inches to 1 mile). Printed on waterproof paper, the route is depicted on seven strip sections, each of which is contained within convenient folds. Additional information (in English, French and German) is provided in separate panels. The only limitation to such a map is the restricted amount of country shown beyond the SDW 'corridor'. However, Harvey's South Downs Way walker's route map is still well worth carrying.

Throughout the guide additional points of information about particularly interesting places and features seen along the Way are highlighted in bold. You'll find a box or side panel close by which expands on the subject. Where the route passes near a source of accommodation or refreshment, this is mentioned.

No timings are given, but for a walk of this length an allowance of 2½ miles for each hour will probably be maintained by most regular walkers.

Bluebells add their touch of magic to downland woods in the springtime

---

Route Symbols on OS maps

	A	Alternative Route
		Route
🚶		Starting point for route east to west
🚶		Starting point for route west to east

For OS symbols key see OS maps

In summer, poppies brighten the way through arable fields

When calculating how long any given stage is likely to take, do not forget to include rests, halts for photography, or time taken to consult the map or guidebook, all of which add substantially to the day's activity. In hot, wet or windy weather, your pace is likely to be slower than normal, so take these conditions into account too.

There is a tendency by some to rush through the countryside with one eye on the hands of the watch, and no time given for contemplation of the intricacies of the landscape, no time to absorb at leisure nature's many gifts – the pleasures that are there for all to enjoy. Walking through the countryside presents so many opportunities it would be a shame to ignore them, for there is more to walking a long-distance path than burning the miles hour after hour. If you open your eyes, heart and mind to the splendours of the world about you, you'll grow richer by the mile. So, as an antedote to the single-minded attitude of getting from A to B as quickly as possible, I've specifically written this guide with a more relaxed outlook in mind, and attempted to bring out the flavour of the walk by including a few anecdotal snippets.

The southern counties do not lend themselves to major epics, but minute by minute along the South Downs Way I experience the wonders of the countryside. In that countryside is revealed the remarkable nature of the ordinary common scenes and pleasures that all may witness when out wandering the footpaths. Noting these little snippets that add much to the eventual sum of life's package of pleasures, it is my hope that those who follow this route will absorb as much of the landscape and the creatures that people it, as possible, and gain as much happiness as I have, each time I've walked it.

As you journey along the South Downs Way, remember it needs your care and respect.

The Country Code

1 Enjoy the countryside and respect its life and work.

2 Guard against all risk of fire.

3 Fasten all gates.

4 Keep dogs under close control.

5 Keep to public paths across farmland.

6 Use gates and stiles to cross fences, hedges and walls.

7 Leave livestock, crops and machinery alone.

8 Take litter home.

9 Help to keep all water clean.

10 Protect wildlife, plants and trees.

11 Take special care on country roads.

12 Make no unnecessary noise.

The Country Code follows in the wake of principles set by Octavia Hill, a champion of the countryside and a co-founder of the National Trust, who wrote in the early days of the 20th century:

Let the grass growing for hay be respected, let the primrose roots be left in their loveliness in the hedges, the birds unmolested and the gates shut. If those who frequented country places would consider those who live there, they would better deserve, and more often retain, the rights and privileges they enjoy.

The Cuckmere's estuary at Cuckmere Haven, with Seaford Head on the far side

STAGE 1

Eastbourne to Alfriston
(Footpath route via the Seven Sisters)

Distance	10½ miles (17km)
Maps	Harvey South Downs Way 1:40,000; OS Landranger 199 Eastbourne & Hastings 1:50,000; OS Explorer 123 South Downs Way, Newhaven to Eastbourne 1:25,000
Accommodation	Eastbourne, Birling Gap, Exceat, Westdean and Alfriston
Refreshments	Eastbourne, Beachy Head, Birling Gap, Exceat, Litlington, Alfriston

Of the two primary stages leading to Alfriston, this route across Beachy Head and the Seven Sisters is not a dedicated bridleway, but is the official walkers' route – the bridleway alternative goes inland via Jevington, and is described as Stage 1(a) below. It is difficult to say which is the finer option for both have much to commend them. So good are the two options, in fact, that it is tempting to walk each one in due course. The clifftop region of Heritage Coast above Eastbourne is scenically dramatic, for the surf froths far below and, as you wander across Beachy Head, you have a lovely view ahead to the Seven Sisters, with Seaford Head beyond the estuary of Cuckmere Haven. The inland route, on the other hand, makes a splendid introduction to the Downs with wide open vistas almost every step of the way, while the little community of Jevington visited mid-journey is a typical flint-walled village with an attractive church in gentle surroundings.

The official route begins on the south-western edge of Eastbourne at Holywell. It then mounts steep, scrub-covered slopes to Beachy Head, continues across to Birling Gap and then tackles the rise and fall of the Seven Sisters. After leaving Haven Brow, the last of the 'Sisters', the route descends gently to the east bank of the Cuckmere, before cutting off and rising once more, this time over sheep-grazed downland to the site of the former Exceat church, then down to the A259 near the Seven Sisters Visitor Centre. A steep hillside leads to Friston Forest where a fine view shows the lazy windings of the Cuckmere below. Westdean is briefly visited, then it's back to forest again. But once the trees have been left behind high farmland takes the route down to Litlington and the banks of the Cuckmere, which makes a gentle companion for the final approach to Alfriston.

Intro 1: To reach the start of the South Downs Way from **Eastbourne** railway station, walk along Grove Road passing the Town Hall, and follow Meads Road through the Meads area of town. At the junction of Beachy Head Road take Meads Street which leads past shops and eventually brings you to King Edward's Parade. The walk begins where Dukes Drive makes a sharp right-hand bend. There's a small café at the foot of a steep slope, and a South Downs Way noticeboard depicting the route (grid ref: 600972).

Intro 2: To reach the start of the South Downs Way from the promenade, head south away from

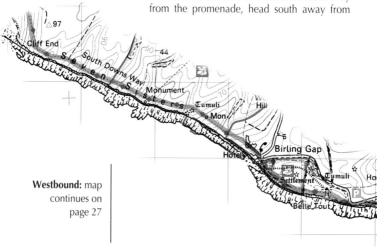

Westbound: map continues on page 27

24

Eastbourne is one of those South Coast resorts that has retained an air of gentility. It's a town of flower beds and bowling greens, a town where Victorian imagery lingers on. The original settlement of East Bourne had a church before the Norman invasion. There were neighbouring hamlets called South Bourne and Sea Houses, the latter a collection of fishermen's cottages, but the three were amalgamated in the mid 19th century, and in 1910 Eastbourne was created a borough. Development as a resort was due largely to the seventh Duke of Devonshire, and it has somehow managed to avoid the tackiness of so many of its coastal neighbours, and discreetly shuns vulgarity. Along the front, north of the pier, stands The Redoubt, a sturdy, circular building – mostly of brick – constructed in the early 1800s as part of the coastal defences against Napoleon. The Wish Tower (see below) also formed part of that defence system.

Eastbourne pier with the sea to your left, walking towards the stumpy **martello tower** ▶ known as the Wish Tower. Beyond it there are neat lawns and flower beds. The promenade continues towards the cliffs and, as the path rises and brings you to a large landscaped mound with seats, bear right to King Edward's Parade. Turn left to Holywell and, when Dukes Drive bends sharply to the right, you see the start of the South Downs Way directly ahead (grid ref: 600972).

The **martello tower**, known as the Wish Tower, is the sole survivor of four such towers originally built along Eastbourne's seafront in 1806–7 to keep Napoleon at bay. During the Napoleonic Wars a whole series of these stocky circular towers were erected along the coastline of Kent and Sussex, and named after the Torre del Martello in Napoleon's homeland of Corsica.

25

Beachy Head is one of the best-known features of the Sussex coast. The clifftop is 536 feet (163m) above the waves, and the red and white ringed lighthouse at its base was built in 1902, the builders and the stone being lowered from the clifftop by cableway. At the start of 1999 a massive rockfall destroyed a section of cliff-face at Beachy Head – a not-so-subtle warning to avoid straying too near the edge. In the severe weather of the early weeks of 2014, more sections of cliff fell into the sea. Britain is shrinking.

Looking east from Haven Brow, the most westerly of the Seven Sisters

Start: At first the Way climbs a steep slope of grass and scrub to a junction of paths. Take the left-hand option among more scrub and gorse, coming out to an open downland above the rim of Whitebread Hole and its playing field. The continuing path winds among bushes of blackthorn, gorse and elder and then, climbing steadily on an old coastguard's path and with splendid views over the sea, approaches **Beachy Head**. Refreshments can be found at the nearby Beachy Head Inn.

Belle Tout **lighthouse** predates that of Beachy Head. Built in 1832 of Aberdeen granite by 'Mad Jack' Fuller, the eccentric squire of Brightling, it served as the lighthouse for this stretch of coast until 1902, but was replaced because the light would often be lost in fog. It has now been converted to a private luxury B&B (www.belletoute.co.uk) with tremendous views in all directions. Following the Beachy Head cliff-fall in 1999, Belle Tout was physically moved a short distance inland.

Continue along the clifftop, but do not stray too close to the edge as the cliffs are crumbling. The Way slopes down almost to road level below the former **lighthouse** of Belle Tout, then rises to pass round the inland side of the enclosing wall. Maintain direction across the cliffs, which were acquired by the National Trust in 1967 and form a designated Heritage Coast, and from which the Seven Sisters can be seen ahead. Before long you arrive at the few buildings and car park at Birling Gap (accommodation, refreshments) (grid ref: 554960).

I was glad then to have chosen to walk westwards, for although the sky was bright and clear, a cold easterly wind was blowing, and I'd rather have that in my back than in my face all day long. On the clifftop walk tiny cowslips were coming into bloom, but few other flowers as yet. Later, and further inland, there would be plenty of colour around my boots, but up here I was well content with views over the sea, with the bleached roller-coaster of the Seven Sisters ahead with their thatch of downland grass, trim and neatly cropped, and recalled previous clifftop wanderings at the end of a variety of long walks. The pleasure to be gained whilst wandering across the Seven Sisters never palls. There's the cry of gulls, the sight, scent and sound of the sea, and broad vistas of the Downs stretching far away inland. I had the wind in my hair and a hundred miles to cover at my own pace. It was good to be back.

A flint track heads past a small toilet block, and soon forks. The way ahead leads to East Dean, but we veer left and through a gate rejoin the

Eastbound: map continues on page 24

27

clifftop path. The route now wanders over the Seven Sisters on a switchback course with the sea glistening below to the left and the green baize of the Downs spreading far off to the right – the Crowlink Estate owned by the National Trust. On the first of the 'Sisters' an obelisk records the dedication of land to the Trust in memory of two brothers killed in the First World War. Next is Baily's Hill, followed by Flat Hill, Flagstaff Brow (another dedication stone), Rough Brow, Short Brow and Haven Brow. Between the 'Sisters' steep, dry valleys, or 'bottoms' can be testing for legs and knees, and the red faces of other walkers betray the effort of each ascent.

From Haven Brow a clear view shows **Cuckmere Haven** below, with Seaford Head on the far side. The Way slopes down and curves to the right and, on reaching the valley bed, goes through a gate and onto a chalk path, the Cuckmere River just to the left. Immediately after crossing a concrete farm road go through a kissing gate and walk up the slope ahead in a north-easterly direction.

Cuckmere Haven is the estuary of the Cuckmere River, a shingle bank guarded by Haven Brow and Seaford Head. In the 15th century it was more open than it is today, for in 1460 raiders from France sailed up the river to Exceat and attacked the village. (Exceat barely exists as a village today.) During the 18th century the Haven was a notorious landing place for smugglers, when contraband goods would be brought upstream to Exceat and Alfriston. As recently as 1923 smugglers were caught there with a haul of expensive brandy. A little inland from the Haven itself an artificial lagoon attracts assorted waders, while the snaking Cuckmere between Exceat and the Haven is busy with swans, tufted ducks, dabchicks, cormorants and herons.

There is little visible sign of a path, but low waymark posts direct the way to another gate on what is almost the highest point. Through this you approach a stone marking the site of the 11th-century church of Exceat, although there's nothing of the building to be seen. The Way now veers a little leftwards, heading north-west

The **Seven Sisters Country Park** spreads east of the Cuckmere River and covers an area of 690 acres. Established in 1971 by East Sussex County Council, but managed by the Sussex Downs Conservation Board, the visitor centre is housed in a converted 18th-century barn at Exceat. The centre has an interesting wildlife and local history exhibition, a shop and toilets. Next door is a convenient restaurant.

where a clear path will be found cutting round the hillside above the Cuckmere's windings, then angles gently down to a gate opposite the **Seven Sisters Visitor Centre** (refreshments, accommodation) (grid ref: 519995).

Cross the A259 with care and wander between a cycle hire building and a cottage, then through a kissing gate and up a steep grass slope, at the top of which a stone stile leads through a wall to the edge of **Friston Forest**. ▶ There's a very fine view from here, out to the Cuckmere's valley easing towards Cuckmere Haven. Take the path ahead among trees, and soon descend more than 200 steps to the hamlet of **Westdean** (accommodation) which is reached beside an attractive duck

Friston Forest covers almost 2000 acres of mainly broad-leaved woodlands. It is owned by South East Water, but managed by the Forestry Commission, and there are several paths and rides through it.

The Cuckmere writhes through its valley on the way to Cuckmere Haven

29

Westdean is a historic little place. It is said that Alfred the Great built a palace here in AD 850, although no trace of it has been found. But there is a charming flint-built rectory dating from the 13th century, and a part-Norman church . Although very small, and with an air of seclusion, Westdean is worth exploring at leisure.

Charleston Manor, on the edge of Friston Forest, is named in the Domesday Book as being owned by William the Conqueror's cup-bearer, Cerlestone. In the grounds the restored tithe barn is all of 177 feet (54m) long, with an enormous tiled roof and a medieval circular dovecote. The gardens are open to the public on set days during the summer.

pond. Continue ahead along a narrow road which becomes a track, and re-enter Friston Forest. Waymarks direct the South Downs Way to the left, but on coming to a junction of tracks, turn right, and when this bears sharp right near the forest edge, the Way goes ahead and descends more steps among trees behind **Charleston Manor.** ◄

The South Downs Way continues along a beech-lined track, then you veer right to cross a stile and follow a hedge. On the downland slopes to the west, a white horse can be seen cut in the chalk above the Cuckmere Valley, on the hill known as High and Over. Eventually come down to the flint-walled village of **Litlington** (refreshments). Turn right in the village street as far as The Plough and Harrow pub. Just beyond this turn left along a narrow footpath leading to a bridge over the Cuckmere.

Accommodation: If you plan to stay overnight at Alfriston Youth Hostel, cross the river here, go up the slope beyond and the hostel is on the right, beside the road (Tel: 0870 770 5666).

The continuing South Downs Way turns right and follows the Cuckmere upstream, passing opposite the Clergy House and Alfriston parish church, to a bridge with white railings where the footpath route joins the bridleway (grid ref: 523031). Cross the bridge and walk ahead up an alleyway which brings you directly into Alfriston High Street (refreshments, accommodation) where you turn right to The Star Inn.

Alfriston is something of a show-piece village, and is one of the busiest in Sussex with day-visitors. It boasts many interesting and picturesque buildings, a number of which have typical downland flint walls. The George Inn (built 1397) is said to have been a smuggler's haunt, while The Star Inn, which dates from the 15th century, bears the figurehead of a Dutch ship that foundered in Cuckmere Haven. The 14th-century church of St Andrew, standing between the greensward of The Tye and the Cuckmere River, is often referred to as 'the Cathedral of the Downs'. Nearby the thatched, half-timbered Clergy House is of similar age to the church, and was the first building bought (in 1896) by the National Trust – for just £10! Alfriston has several shops, restaurants, pubs and tearooms, and a choice of accommodation.

Litlington is tucked under the Downs on the east bank of the Cuckmere, its small Norman church wearing a white weatherboarded bell-tower and a shingled cap. Next door Church Farm is also very old, and has Caen stone in its walls, which leads some to suggest it may have been a priest's house. The name of the village is derived from 'Lytela's farmstead' and is pronounced Lillington.

STAGE 1(a)

Eastbourne to Alfriston
(Bridleway route inland via Jevington)

Distance	8 miles (12½km)
Maps	Harvey South Downs Way 1:40,000; OS Landranger 199 Eastbourne & Hastings 1:50,000; OS Explorer 123 South Downs Way, Newhaven to Eastbourne 1:25,000
Accommodation	Eastbourne, Jevington, Wilmington (+1 mile), Milton Street (+¾ mile), Alfriston
Refreshments	Eastbourne, Jevington, Alfriston

The bridleway alternative to the Seven Sisters route is a delightful stage among rolling downland which affords wide views and with plenty of interest throughout. In many respects it is as rewarding as the official footpath stage described above, albeit of a completely different nature, and is highly recommended. It begins on the edge of Eastbourne where the Seven Sisters route begins, but immediately heads inland (soon rising onto the Downs), briefly crosses a golf course overlooking Eastbourne and the distant Pevensey Levels, and heads north before descending a clear track among gorse bushes and banks of wild flowers, into a narrow valley with Jevington neatly spaced within its confines. A tree-shaded climb leads onto the Downs again and, at Windover Hill, the route journeys across the unseen head of England's largest chalk figure, the Long Man of Wilmington. More expansive views entice across the Cuckmere's gap towards Bostal Hill and Firle Beacon, and northward into the flat open spaces of the Weald. A winding chalk track snakes down to the Cuckmere's valley, then the bridleway edges water meadows before joining the footpath route for a crossing of the Cuckmere into Alfriston.

Start: The SDW bridleway begins at Eastbourne's south-western end, where Duke's Drive, the B2103, makes a sharp bend at the foot of a prominent slope of downland (grid ref: 600972). A small café ('The Kiosk') is conveniently situated here. For directions on how to reach it from the town, see Stage 1.

While the footpath route to Alfriston via Beachy Head and the Seven Sisters strikes directly up the slope, the bridleway route heads to the right, rising gently just above the road and keeping to the foot of the slope, before swinging left to rise through a grassy gully. Above the 'gully' the way continues between island-like groups of trees, making for the head of the slope where there's a 4-way crossing of grass trails. Turn sharp right and contour along the open Downs with a view overlooking Eastbourne and the coastline which curves in the distance towards Bexhill and Hastings.

In another ½ mile cross the B2103 (**caution!**) near its junction with a road heading for Beachy Head and Birling Gap. Over the road bear left and continue heading north alongside trees until these curve to the right. Now go up the slope ahead to briefly join a stony track leading past a dew pond and a trig point. Pass these to your right and shortly after come to a junction with another bridleway. Keep ahead, and before long you'll reach the A259 at grid ref: 585985.

Accommodation: Eastbourne Youth Hostel is situated about a third of a mile downhill to the right.

Cross the road with care and take the broad track opposite, through a golf course. The track is easy to follow and it leads for a little over 2½ miles to Jevington. There are fine views almost all the way. At first these extend across the low-lying Pevensey Levels to the right, while to the left East Dean sprawls in its hollow, with Friston water tower projecting thumb-like above it. The Way passes **a dew pond** ▶ and ¾ mile later comes to crossing tracks at Bourne Hill (grid ref: 577009). Just above to the right is a trig point, and on the mound which marks

Dew Ponds are seen in many parts of the South Downs. Because of the permeable nature of chalk, there is practically no natural surface water, so saucer-shaped scoops have been dug out and in many places given a concrete base (clay was originally used) to trap and contain rainwater for grazing animals. Traditionally these dew ponds were known as 'cloud ponds', 'mist ponds' or, more prosaically, 'sheep ponds'.

33

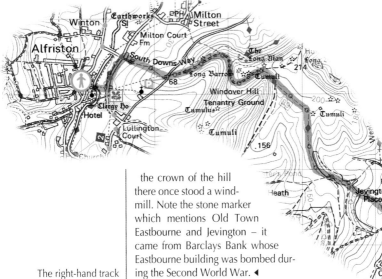

the crown of the hill there once stood a windmill. Note the stone marker which mentions Old Town Eastbourne and Jevington – it came from Barclays Bank whose Eastbourne building was bombed during the Second World War. ◄

The right-hand track here is the route of the **Wealdway**.

Ignoring alternatives to right and left continue ahead, now descending beside clumps of gorse on what becomes a delightful sunken track with a preview of Jevington snug in its valley below. The banks are lavish with flowers in springtime – cowslips, bugle, and wild raspberry canes straggling by the fence. Cowslips are symbolic of the Downs, and these lovely yellow-headed plants will be seen in abundance throughout the walk in late springtime. The name originates from the belief that the flower would appear wherever there was a cowpat! For centuries it was used as an ingredient in the making of vinegar, mead, wine and even cheese.

A luxurious fold of downland spreads in gentle curves on all sides. Pausing to take it all in I recognised the shape of Combe Hill to the north where I had crossed

The **Wealdway** is a long-distance recreational route which travels 82 miles (132km) from the bank of the River Thames at Gravesend in Kent, to the clifftop at Beachy Head. On the way it crosses the North Downs, several High Weald ridges, Ashdown Forest, the expanse of the Weald and, finally, the South Downs.

one glorious late-spring afternoon a couple of years ago when walking the Wealdway. I remembered it well: the peace, the views, the sunshine. Now I had the peace of a spring morning, more fine views and sunshine too. Ahead, Jevington sank into a crease of hills. Behind it a sloping meadow on the Downs had recently been rolled in stripes, as though a welcome carpet had been laid out for my arrival. In one such meadow horses were grazing. In another the lazy drift of sheep shuffled patterns of white on green. Happiness, I thought, is something we're seldom aware of until it has passed. But wandering down the track towards Jevington with

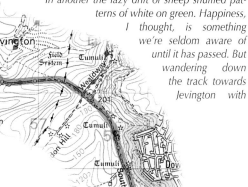

the sun on my neck, I knew there was nowhere else I'd rather be, and nothing I'd rather be doing than setting off on a 100-mile walk across those Downs. Ambling down the track to Jevington, I was happy. And knew it.

Jevington is a quiet, back-country downland village that was once a smugglers' haunt. The flint-walled church of St Andrew has an impressive Saxon tower 1000 years old, in which there is a bell said to have been brought ashore from a shipwreck. The remainder of the building dates from the 13th century, but there are Roman bricks in its construction. The Hungry Monk restaurant opposite the lane leading to the church is where the banoffeepie was invented in 1972!

St Andrew's Church in Jevington has a fine Saxon tower

On reaching **Jevington** (accommodation, refreshments) turn right along the road and about 50 yards later bear left on the approach to the church. Continue beyond the Saxon church of St Andrew along a narrowing enclosed bridleway where a signpost indicates 'Alfriston 3 miles'. Soon the Way rises among horse chestnut, elm, ash and elder, crosses another track and shortly joins a more prominent path which continues up the slope – beside which wild garlic and bluebells mass in spring. At Holt Brow emerge from trees to a

crossing path. Turn right and within a few yards go through a bridle gate. Maintain direction along the edge of a field, and through a second gate come to a large open grassland.

There is a sudden awareness of space as you emerge onto the bare crest of the Downs. There are far views to the sea but, much closer, downland folds into the green coomb of Deep Dean. The ruined walls of Hill Barn give rise to speculation as to their origin.

Several low waymark posts guide the route across this downland plateau before a clear chalk path leads along the top edge of Deep Dean to another gate (grid ref: 544034). Passing through, veer left. The lip of the escarpment is now to your right, and should you venture to it you notice **Wilmington** far below, Arlington Reservoir beyond that and the immense levels of the Weald spreading to a distant blue line of Ashdown Forest. Although you will not see it from this point, you are virtually standing on the head of the Long Man of Wilmington. The Cuckmere River snakes out of the Weald, and to the west you gaze across the broad valley it has cut through the Downs, to the rise of Bostal Hill and Firle Beacon where the South Downs Way passes on Stage 2.

Now heading south-west the grassy trail passes along the left-hand side of various earthworks on Windover Hill (two or three burial barrows and ditches, and mounds that indicate refuse pits from Stone Age flint

Wilmington is famous for the Long Man, said to be England's largest chalk figure, which stands 226 feet (69m) long and, with a stave in each hand, overlooks the ruins of a Benedictine priory founded in 1100. No-one knows quite how old the Long Man is although it has been suggested that he dates from the Bronze Age, about 4000 years ago. Both he and the priory ruins are now in the care of the Sussex Archaeological Trust. The parish church next door to the priory has a weatherboarded bell-tower topped with a shingle spire, and is as old as the priory, while an enormous yew tree in the churchyard is thought to be 1600 years old. The pendulous branches are supported by wooden props and chains.

Unseen from the SDW, the route crosses above the Long Man of Wilmington

mines). Beyond the summit of Windover Hill the route winds to the right and then left, descending a sunken track, formerly a coach road, round the head of another dry valley (Ewe Dean).

Accommodation: If you plan to find accommodation in Wilmington, take the right-hand option when the track forks. At crossing tracks turn right on a path that cuts along the flank of hillside to the foot of the Long Man. Now bear left on an enclosed path which leads to a narrow lane. Bear right into Wilmington.

The track takes you past an underground reservoir and eventually spills onto a country lane. Cross straight over and continue down a narrow, sunken track among blackthorn and a line of elms, until coming to a road junction.

Accommodation: For accommodation in Milton Street, turn right here.

Cross slightly left ahead and enter a meadow, then turn left and, remaining parallel with the road, keep along the edge of the meadow with Alfriston church seen ahead, the Cuckmere off to the right, hidden below a grass embankment. At the end of the meadow go through a gate and turn right along a metalled path. As you come to a white-railed footbridge you join the footpath route from the Seven Sisters. On the Alfriston side of the bridge the bridleway bears right in front of cottages, then left between flint walls to reach the Market Cross in the High Street (accommodation, refreshments) (grid ref: 520032). Now head to the left along the street as far as the The Star Inn. For more information about Alfriston, please refer to the end of Stage 1, footpath route.

STAGE 2
Alfriston to Southease

Distance	7 miles (11km)
Maps	Harvey South Downs Way 1:40,000; OS Landranger 199 Eastbourne & Hastings 1:50,000; OS Explorer 123 South Downs Way, Newhaven to Eastbourne and 122 South Downs Way, Steyning to Newhaven 1:25,000
Accommodation	Alciston (+1 mile), Firle (+1 mile), Southease, Rodmell, Telscombe (+1¼ miles)
Refreshments	Café at South Downs YHA, Southease.

This stage mounts the northern crest of the Downs for a lovely walk on smooth grass speckled with flowers, among sites of ancient history where long barrows roughen the turf, and where a remote Saxon cemetery holds the secrets of a past age remote from the technology of the 21st century. From Alfriston's busy heart the route climbs to Bostal Hill where the summer skies are bright with multi-coloured paragliders. Then on to Firle Beacon, 713 feet (217m) above the sea, whose crown has been cropped by generations of Southdown sheep. The Downs then curve westward, and the trail crosses Beddingham Hill beside a pair of lofty radio masts to reach Itford Hill overlooking the River Ouse. A winding descent comes to Itford Farm and the Newhaven road, and once across the river you enter the tiny village of Southease.

As there is no availability of refreshment on this stage until you cross the A26 shortly before reaching Southease, it is advisable to carry supplies from Alfriston.

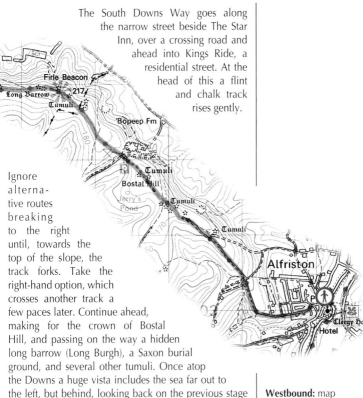

The South Downs Way goes along the narrow street beside The Star Inn, over a crossing road and ahead into Kings Ride, a residential street. At the head of this a flint and chalk track rises gently.

Ignore alternative routes breaking to the right until, towards the top of the slope, the track forks. Take the right-hand option, which crosses another track a few paces later. Continue ahead, making for the crown of Bostal Hill, and passing on the way a hidden long barrow (Long Burgh), a Saxon burial ground, and several other tumuli. Once atop the Downs a huge vista includes the sea far out to the left, but behind, looking back on the previous stage of the route, the Long Man of Wilmington is hidden from view, but the rolling downland wall is clearly seen above both Wilmington and Alfriston, stretching southward to Cuckmere Haven. The Weald is a low-lying contrast with Berwick (a neat corner worth searching out on another occasion), huddled in an expanse of green.

Striding towards Bostal Hill my attention was caught by what appeared to be a mass of giant butterflies drifting in the breeze, but on drawing closer revealed themselves to be paragliders, each brightly coloured arc of silk supporting a speck of man or woman competing with

Westbound: map continues on page 43

A spur of land by Bostal Hill makes a splendid vantage point from which to study the Weald

the larks for a privileged overview of the Downs and the Weald. I counted 17 in all, spiralling, drifting, soaring – hanging in the sky and connected with the earth only by their shadows.

Across Bostal Hill the trail comes to a small car park, and beyond this maintains direction for ¾ mile to Firle Beacon, which is marked by a trig point from which there's another immense panorama to enjoy (grid ref: 485059).

Accommodation: Just beyond the trig point an alternative path descends to West Firle (or Firle as it is known), and is the one to take if you plan to find accommodation there.

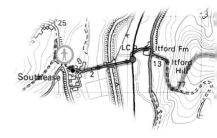

The Way now curves westward aiming towards lofty radio masts on Beddingham Hill nearly 2 miles away – as the route passes below them they form a convenient marker. Between Firle Beacon and the radio masts the Way goes through another small car park, this one giving road access to **Firle** seen at the foot of the Downs.

Firle, shown as West Firle on OS maps, is a compact village nestling below the Downs. The elegant Firle Place, which stands near the church with woodland behind, was originally built in 1557, but then rebuilt nearly 200 years later – the Georgian outer retaining the Tudor core. To the east of Firle Place stands the round folly of Firle Tower, which is clearly seen from the Downs near Firle Beacon. Charleston Farmhouse, further east again, became a centre for the Bloomsbury Group of writers and artists after being discovered in 1916 by Virginia and Leonard Woolf. The house now contains work by Virginia's sister, Vanessa Bell, and Duncan Grant who died in 1978.

Around us now are more prehistoric sites – round barrows and ancient settlements. There was an Iron Age village near Firle Beacon, a Bronze Age collection of huts and workshops west of Beddingham Hill. North of the escarpment, and on the outskirts of Glynde, there was an Iron Age hill fort on Mount Caburn. For more than 300 years it was occupied and active, until the Romans came. Roman trackways crossed the Downs above Firle as part of an important trade route. Grain would have been carted along these tracks bound for the coast where

Eastbound:
map continues
on page 41

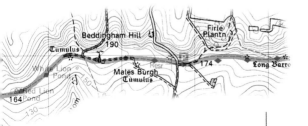

Seaford and Newhaven stand today. On these Downs, 'broad and bare to the skies', only a handful of modern cars, a few model aircraft and the twin radio masts ahead represent a world so very different to that experienced by the first settlers of these green sweeping crests. Yet with imagination it is possible to stir the spirits of our wind-blown ancestors, and share with them the empty miles.

Pass along the right-hand side of the masts. The track then veers a little to the right and goes through a gate by a narrow metalled road. Cross through another gate directly ahead and wander parallel with the left-hand fence towards Itford Hill, eventually passing a trig point and a dried-up dew pond known as Red Lion Pond on your right (grid ref: 446055).

From here to the valley of the Ouse the downland is rich in wild flowers, with views stretching from Newhaven out to the left where the Ouse spills into the sea, to Lewes and Mount Caburn off to the right. On reaching the lip of the Downs, Itford Farm is seen below to the west, beside the A26. The slope plunges steeply, but the Way swings left and descends to a footbridge spanning the busy road. Over this curve right towards Itford Farm. You have now reached the South Downs Youth Hostel and its Courtyard Café. Even if you do not plan to stay at the hostel, the café is open to the general public daily between 10.00 and 16.00. ◄

The farm lane crosses the railway line at the halt of Southease Station, then a short distance beyond comes to the River Ouse. This is contained between sturdy banks and is crossed by road bridge. The reedy ditches beyond form a lively habitat for frogs and toads, and heron are sometimes seen stalking for a meal.

Alternative route: The main South Downs Way continues along the lane into Southease, but an optional alternative, which misses the hamlet, visits Rodmell instead and would be useful for anyone planning to spend the night there (although there is a shorter and more direct road route to Rodmell mentioned in Stage 3 below).

YHA South Downs was opened in 2013 on the site of Itford Farm, which dates back to the 13th century. Open throughout the year, the hostel has 88 beds in twin/double rooms and dormitories, a self-contained cottage and camping facilities (Tel: 01273 858780).

Take the riverside path on the right, immediately after crossing the bridge, and walk downstream for about a mile. On coming to a track (bridleway) turn left and follow this into **Rodmell.** ▶ To rejoin the South Downs Way walk along Mill Lane, which starts from the main road near the Abergavenny Arms, initially between cottages. The lane narrows and becomes a private road (but public bridleway) with fields on the left folding down into Cricketing Bottom. Near the crest of the hill, by the entrance to Mill Hill (grid ref: 413054), turn right on an enclosed bridleway running parallel with the garden boundary. This is the route of the South Downs Way.

Main walk continued: Keep on the lane and, about 400 yards beyond the bridge, you enter the hamlet of Southease near the village green.

Accommodation: If you plan to spend the night at Telscombe Youth Hostel follow directions given in Stage 3: Southease to Housedean.

Southease consists of a few 17th-century cottages, a village green and an attractive church with a rare circular tower built in the 12th century (there are only three such towers in Sussex, all of which are in the Ouse Valley), and some faded, medieval wall paintings. Southease was first recorded in a charter of AD 966 granting the church and manor – and that of nearby Telscombe – to Hyde Abbey in Winchester. Southease was then 'Sueise' and the charter, made by the Anglo-Saxon King Edgar (Eadgar), included 28 hides of land. In the Domesday Book of 1086 the village rated 27 hides and 'the villeins are assessed for 38,500 herrings and at £4 for porpoises.' This reference to herrings and porpoises gives an indication of the importance of Southease as a fishery. At the time the Ouse was a major tidal river, and it is thought possible that the lake in the grounds of Southease Place may have once been a harbour.

Rodmell is best known for Monks House, the home of Virginia and Leonard Woolf (see Firle), which is now in the ownership of the National Trust. They came here in 1919, but in 1941 Virginia, suffering mental illness, walked down to the River Ouse and committed suicide. Rodmell has a Norman church and some attractive cottages. Southwest of the village, on the route of the South Downs Way, there used to stand a windmill, and the Abergavenny Arms pub beside the main road is named after the Marquess of Abergavenny who, until just after the First World War, was the principal landowner.

STAGE 3
Southease to Housedean (A27)

Distance	6 miles (9½km)
Maps	Harvey South Downs Way 1:40,000; OS Landranger 198 Brighton & Lewes 1:50,000; OS Explorer 122 South Downs Way, Steyning to Newhaven 1:25,000
Accommodation	Rodmell (+½ mile), Telscombe (+1¼ miles), Kingston (+½ mile), Lewes (+1½–2 miles)
Refreshments	None on the route

On this stage the route jurneys over another broad, exposed downland ridge heading north-west over Mill Hill, Front Hill, Iford Hill (not to be confused with Itford Hill of the last stage), then along the scarp edge of Swanborough Hill overlooking neat villages tucked against the foot of the Downs. There are more dew ponds, the site of a one-time windmill, and a stretch along Juggs Road, a track formerly used by fish traders travelling from Brighton to Lewes. Brighton is kept at bay well to the west as the South Downs Way curves round the head of Cold Coombes then descends alongside Newmarket Plantation to the A27. Once across this busy road, walkers seeking accommodation could catch a bus into Lewes.

On a calm and sunny day this makes a gorgeous walk. Larks rise from the fields to trill overhead. There will, no doubt, be pheasants and hares sharing the track; there are badger setts along Swanborough Hill, foxes in Newmarket Plantation, and wild flowers set in the downland turf. There are no refreshment facilities at all along the way, and no habitation between Mill Hill and the A27. But views there are in plenty.

Passing Southease church on your left, walk up the tree-lined lane to a road junction where you turn right. After a few paces another lane cuts left, signposted to Telscombe. At the entrance to this lane you will find a gate on the northern side leading into a meadow.

> **Accommodation:** If you need accommodation in Rodmell do not go through this gate, but remain on the road heading north for ½ mile. This brings you to the village.

Once in the meadow go briefly down the slope, then bear right through a little area of trees and continue down to a farm track. Bear left and wander through the dry valley known as Cricketing Bottom for a little over ½ mile. About 100 yards before the track reaches a group of farm buildings the Way turns sharply to the right.

> **Accommodation:** The continuing track leads to Telscombe for youth hostel accommodation. Go between the farm buildings and continue south-west for ½ mile or so. The track then swings left through a

Telscombe youth hostel, a row of converted cottages a little over a mile from the South Downs Way

gate, and curves uphill to a narrow lane. Keep ahead along the lane and you come shortly to Telscombe. The youth hostel stands next to the church.

After turning away from the track near the farm buildings, the Way hugs the foot of the slope, goes through a gate, then climbs Mill Hill to gain views of Seaford Head to the south-east. At the crown of the hill come onto a drive at the entrance to a house (Mill Hill) and cross directly ahead, joining the alternative route from

Rodmell described in Stage 2 (grid ref: 413054). The bridleway follows the garden boundary fence, then continues ahead with another wide view which includes Lewes off to the right.

For a little over 1½ miles the route makes a steady course over the typical farmed downland of Front Hill and Iford Hill. It is wide open country up here – open to the breezes, open to the sun, with neither shade nor shelter. Passing through occasional gates the

Way then follows a concrete farm road cutting through prairie-like fields.

Mid-morning April sun beamed down and washed my shadow into the young spring corn. Out of that flint-cluttered field rose one lark after another, thrashing the air with their wings they sang as they soared higher and higher, intent on distracting my attention from their nests. What gifts their songs were for a solitary walker! Then over the brow of the hill ahead came three tracksuited athletes chatting as they ran. (Lord knows where they found the breath to talk.) Within a matter of moments they were past me and pounding the concrete on the downhill slope to Mill Hill. I was relieved when they disappeared from sight, for this was a landscape that needed no human interruption. These Downs belonged to the birds and animals. Alone, I could absorb their strengths and their frailties, their past and present, their own personal songs and scents. Alone, one could share their secrets and be glad for the day. I was well content to be on my own.

After a long stretch of concrete the farm road veers hard left towards a large barn. Leave the road at this point and head off to the right for about 60 yards, then go through a gate into a sloping meadow. Turn left and keep to the top of the slope, soon joining a farm track where you maintain direction. It is a pleasant stretch to travel along – one of the best for many a long mile – for your attention is constantly being drawn

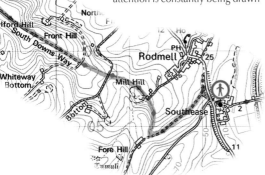

The Way follows a clear track along the flank of Swanborough Hill

down the flanks of the hills, rucked here and there by steep coombs, to the villages of Iford and Kingston-near-Lewes, with the substantial buildings of Swanborough Manor (dating from the 12th century) in between.

When the track cuts sharply to the left (where the bridleway of Breach Road crosses), continue ahead and go through a bridle gate onto a broad grassland hilltop. There is little sign of a track here, but you maintain direction and pass to the left of Kingston Hill dew pond (grid ref: 383078), surrounded by gorse . Before long come to a second dew pond, also marked by gorse bushes, but this one lies just left of the Way. It was here that Ashcombe Windmill used to spin its six sweeps (or sails) to the wind. You are now on the line of **Juggs Road**, although there's little to show for it on the ground.

Pass through the gate and head south-westward keeping parallel with the right-hand fence, beyond which the scarp slope dips towards the busy A27 a mile and a world away. Contrast that with the cowslips at your feet and the song of larks high above! Near the end of this long meadow veer leftwards to find another bridle gate. Through this turn half-right and follow another

Juggs Road is a one-time trading route across the South Downs used by fisher-folk from Brighton. 'Juggs' was the name given to these traders by the people of Lewes, supposedly from the earthenware jugs, or pots, in which the fish were salted and kept fresh. These traders regularly carted their fish by donkey along this route to market in the county town.

fence. The South Downs Way now slopes downhill on the western side of Cold Coombes, soon gaining a clear view across this fine rich downland. The Way passes alongside the beechwood of Newmarket Plantation then, passing through two or three more gates, leads beneath a railway arch, emerging near the A27. Now the Way turns hard left between fences and comes to a minor road. Go up this and across the A27 on a bridge, then bear right to pass alongside the grey, square building of Housedean Farm (grid ref: 369092).

Accommodation: Should you be in need of accommodation, continue beyond the farm alongside the road to where a bus stop has a frequent service to Lewes.

STAGE 4
Housedean (A27) to Pyecombe

Distance	8½ miles (13½km)
Maps	Harvey South Downs Way 1:40,000; OS Landranger 198 Brighton & Lewes 1:50,000; OS Explorer 122 South Downs Way, Steyning to Newhaven 1:25,000
Accommodation	Plumpton (+¾ mile), Ditchling (+1¾ miles), Keymer (+1½ miles) Clayton, Pyecombe
Refreshments	None on the route until Pyecombe

Between the heavy traffic of the A27 outside Lewes and the A23 at Pyecombe, the South Downs provide an oasis of calm, and reward with birdsong and the bleating of sheep. Much of this stretch of the Downs has been put to the plough, arable replacing pasture, but around Ditchling Beacon the downland is protected as a nature reserve and it remains much as it would have been for centuries. Wide views become commonplace, but earlier, in a 'back-country' of folded hills blocked by woodland crowns, you lose all sense of height and spaciousness as the route leads between large fields with no plunging scarp slope to draw perspective.

It is an historic area with a number of ancient sites along the way. During the first part, beyond Balmer Down, the track passes west of flower-rich Mount Harry where, in 1264, Simon de Montfort took arms against Henry III in the Battle of Lewes, the outcome of which led to our present parliamentary system. On Plumpton Plain is the site of a Bronze Age settlement. In Ditchling village, below the Downs, the Romans had a fortified camp. (Stretches of Roman road may still be detected traversing west-east at the foot of the Downs.)

The initial part of the route from Housedean Farm and the A27 replaces the former trail which led through Ashcombe Plantation. Now the Way climbs Long Hill, goes through Bunkershill Plantation and rejoins the 'old' route in the arable fields of Balmer Down. The Downs of sheep-grazed grassland are to be found on Plumpton Plain with the trail heading west to Ditchling Beacon, where the South Downs Way reaches its highest point in Sussex, but where solitude is rare. Less than 2 miles later a pair of windmills rise out of the fields ahead – Jack and Jill, the well-known Clayton Windmills. Skirting these to the south, a track slopes downhill beside a golf course and comes to the main road a short distance from Pyecombe.

*Ditchling Beacon is
a protected
nature reserve*

Heading east alongside the flint wall which surrounds Housedean Farm, turn left when the wall ends, ascend some steps and, going through a gate, continue up a sloping field to Long Hill. The head of the slope coincides with the top of the field, and in the left-hand corner another gate gives access to the woodland shown on the map as Bunkershill Plantation. The bridleway soon begins to descend quite steeply, and on emerging from the woods, it swings to the right between fences. At the end of this fence-enclosed section come to a crossing path and turn left.

There follows a lengthy stretch as you rise gently along the arable slopes of Balmer Down for a mile or so, passing a dew pond on the right and, later, going beneath a line of power cables you come to a crossing track and bear right. This bridlepath leads away from arable land, takes you between hedges and alongside a small woodland before coming to a farm track where you turn left (grid ref: 370125). To the right of this turning is the National Trust downland of Blackcap.

Very soon you come to the scarp edge along Plumpton Plain, with a Wealden panorama to enjoy stretching far to the north. The village of Plumpton is clearly seen below with the extensive buildings of its agricultural college, the glimmer of a lake at 16th-century Plumpton Place and, further north, the outline of Plumpton racecourse.

Accommodation: A little under a mile after turning along Plumpton Plain is a track heading off to the

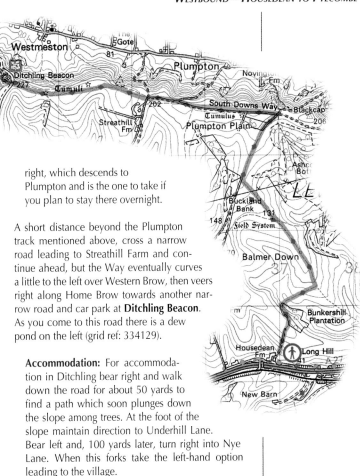

right, which descends to Plumpton and is the one to take if you plan to stay there overnight.

A short distance beyond the Plumpton track mentioned above, cross a narrow road leading to Streathill Farm and continue ahead, but the Way eventually curves a little to the left over Western Brow, then veers right along Home Brow towards another narrow road and car park at **Ditchling Beacon**. As you come to this road there is a dew pond on the left (grid ref: 334129).

Accommodation: For accommodation in Ditchling bear right and walk down the road for about 50 yards to find a path which soon plunges down the slope among trees. At the foot of the slope maintain direction to Underhill Lane. Bear left and, 100 yards later, turn right into Nye Lane. When this forks take the left-hand option leading to the village.

Ditchling Beacon, the highest of the South Downs in Sussex, is owned by the National Trust, with a nature reserve in the care of the Sussex Wildlife Trust. The summit is surrounded by the rectangular outline of an Iron Age hill fort.

Go through the car park (there is usually an ice cream van here in summer) and keep ahead, passing a little to the right of the trig point (813feet/248m). The Way leads through a nature reserve, passes another dew pond and, little more than a mile from Ditchling Beacon, edges past a tall wooden signpost known as the Keymer Post which marks the boundary between East and West Sussex.

Accommodation: For accommodation in Keymer take the right-hand path here.

Jill, one of the Clayton Windmills, is a prominent feature on the Downs

Just beyond this the first sighting of the **Clayton Windmills** is made, rising out of the fields ahead. Shortly before the windmills you come to a crossing track and turn left.

Accommodation: To find accommodation in Clayton do not turn left, but go ahead on the track, then take a path on the right which leads round the side of the first windmill (Jack). This continues past the second mill (Jill) and descends to Underhill Lane, Clayton.

The **Clayton Windmills** (Jack and Jill) are a much-loved feature of the South Downs. Jack, the upper, black-painted smock mill built in 1866, has been converted to a private residence and was once the home of Henry Longhurst, the golfer, but Jill, the gleaming white post mill, is in the care of a preservation society and is open to the public most Sundays 14.00–17.00 between May and September, with a tearoom providing refreshments. Built in 1821, Jill originally stood in Patcham, Brighton, but was towed by oxen to her present site, where she worked until 1906. For further information see www.jillwindmill.org.uk.

The track leads between buildings at New Barn Farm and, 100 yards later, at crossing tracks, you turn right on an enclosed bridleway alongside a golf course. Sloping downhill, eventually pass to the right of the clubhouse and come to the A273 Haywards Heath to Brighton road. Cross with care and bear left on a narrow bush-enclosed path leading into Pyecombe (accommodation, refreshments). Turn right into School Lane and soon reach the parish church (grid ref: 292126).

Pyecombe is a small village wedged between the A273 and A23. Its flint and pebbledash Norman church has a squat 13th-century tower and, inside, a finely decorated lead font. The tapsell, or pintle, gate which leads into the churchyard has a shepherd's crook as its latch – the village is famed for the manufacture of these crooks which were used by shepherds throughout the South Downs. In 1603 the original village was hit by plague.

STAGE 5

Pyecombe to Botolphs (Adur Valley)

Distance	7½ miles (12km)
Maps	Harvey South Downs Way 1:40,000; OS Landranger 198 Brighton & Lewes 1:50,000; OS Explorer 122 South Downs Way, Steyning to Newhaven 1:50,000
Accommodation	Poynings (+¾ mile), Edburton (+½ mile), Truleigh Hill Youth Hostel, Bramber (+1½ miles), Steyning (+½–1½ miles)
Refreshments	Saddlescombe, Devil's Dyke

This part of the route is broken into two distinct stages. The first short leg climbs out of Pyecombe to cross West Hill, then descends to a farm and cottages at Saddlescombe which is, in true geographical terms, set at a saddle, or pass, in a coombe. Ahead rises the scrub- and tree-covered Devil's Dyke, where the second stage of the route returns to the back of the Downs once more. West of Devil's Dyke the Way leads across the Fulking escarpment on a regular rise and fall of hills, often with distant views blinkered by higher ground to the north. Over the cluttered summit of Truleigh Hill the track carries the South Downs Way down to the Shoreham road, then over the River Adur to meet the end of the Downs Link path near St Botolph's Church.

From Pyecombe church walk ahead along Church Hill (not Church Lane), soon sloping downhill to a slip road where you bear left to cross the A23 by the road bridge. Turn left and, almost opposite The Plough Inn, bear right. Just beyond Hobbs Cottage go uphill on a chalk track, passing through a bridle gate. Halfway up the slope go through another gate where a sign announces Newtimber Hill, owned by the National Trust. Maintain direction to the top of the hill, then veer right alongside a fence From here you can see the tall buildings of Brighton to the south and, back the way you have come, the Clayton Windmills. As you progress and go through yet another gate, so the Devil's Dyke shows itself clearly ahead, with the tall radio masts of Truleigh Hill beyond that.

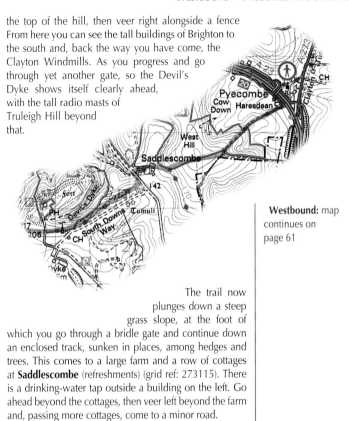

Westbound: map continues on page 61

The trail now plunges down a steep grass slope, at the foot of which you go through a bridle gate and continue down an enclosed track, sunken in places, among hedges and trees. This comes to a large farm and a row of cottages at **Saddlescombe** (refreshments) (grid ref: 273115). There is a drinking-water tap outside a building on the left. Go ahead beyond the cottages, then veer left beyond the farm and, passing more cottages, come to a minor road.

Saddlescombe, near the Devil's Dyke, has been farmed since before the 13th century, when it came into the ownership of the Knights Templar. In 1995 Saddlescombe Farm was acquired by the National Trust. In addition to 500 acres of agricultural land, it has several unspoiled Sussex farm buildings which include a blacksmith's forge complete with furnace and bellows. There is also a campsite and the Hiker's Rest café (closed on Wednesdays), which provides welcome refreshments. For more information visit www.nationaltrust.org.uk/ saddlescombe-farm-and-newtimber-hill.

Accommodation: For accommodation in Poynings take the footpath that parallels the road to the right.

Cross to a broad track and go through a gate at the foot of the slope to enter Summer Down. The Way climbs well to the left of the dry valley of **Devil's Dyke**, curves to the right alongside railings which enclose an underground reservoir, and then forks. Take the

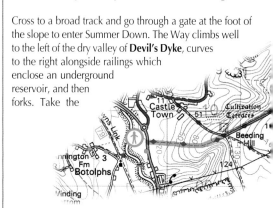

right-hand alternative which hugs the lower edge of a sloping grassland before easing uphill to a major crossing path. Turn right. The path winds among trees and bushes, nearly always with the red-brick Devil's Dyke Hotel (refreshments) in view. Eventually come onto the narrow lane which leads to the hotel. Cross to a gate providing access onto a broad, open downland,

The **Devil's Dyke** covers 183 acres of downland, but the name refers to the steep dry valley – the largest single coombe of chalk karst in Britain – cut into it. According to local legend the Devil attempted to carve a dyke through the Downs to enable the sea to flood the churches of the Weald. Working at night he shovelled the earth into great mounds, but was disturbed by an old lady carrying a candle, which he mistook for the dawn. The earth mounds are the tumuli and massive Iron Age hill fort on the summit, and the whole area is now in the care of the National Trust. Since 1987 the Trust has been running a South Downs Appeal which has seen the purchase of a number of important sites. Here in the Devil's Dyke the chalk grassland, dotted with scrub, provides a habitat for the nationally uncommon Scarce Forester moth and the Adonis Blue butterfly, while the native flora includes several orchids (among them Bee, Fragrant, Twayblade and Common Spotted), as well as wild thyme, horseshoe vetch and birdsfoot trefoil.

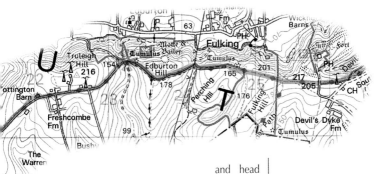

                                                          and head
            towards the radio masts of Truleigh Hill,
        passing well to the left of a trig point and the
earthen ramparts of another Iron Age hill fort.

Eastbound: map
continues on
page 59

The Way leads along Fulking escarpment, passes a
Bronze Age burial barrow and then, descending Perching
Hill, dips below power cables to a crossing track (Fulking
to the right, Southwick to the left). The Way continues
ahead on an obvious chalk track sweeping between
pastures on the way to Edburton Hill and Truleigh Hill.
Pass alongside the large buildings and masts that are an
unfortunate eyesore, and maintaining direction come
to Truleigh Hill Youth Hostel (accommodation) which
stands beside the track to the right (grid ref: 221107).

Continue beyond the hostel, and you will soon find
a narrow footpath running parallel with the track/lane
along its right-hand side. Now you should be able to see
the clump of trees of Chanctonbury Ring on the edge of
the downland scarp about 5 miles to the west. When the
lane makes a sharp left-hand bend, go ahead through a
bridle gate to follow a meadowland path which leads
to a second gate. Through this an enclosed bridleway
descends to the A283 Shoreham road about ½ mile
south of Upper Beeding (grid ref: 197096).

Accommodation: From here buses serve Shoreham
and Brighton in one direction, and Steyning and
Bramber in the other.

Truleigh Hill Youth Hostel stands beside the SDW on the crest of the Downs above the Adur's valley

The **Downs Link**, as its name suggests, is a 34-mile (55km) recreational route between the North and South Downs, which follows for much of its length the bed of a dismantled railway. It begins on St Martha's Hill near Guildford, and ends at Botolphs.

Bear left along the road for nearly 150 yards, then cross with care to a lay-by and an enclosed path. In a few paces come to a water tap, trough, a few seats and a sign indicating 7 miles to Washington. The Way now crosses a footbridge over the River Adur, then bears right alongside the river. About 150 yards further on it swings left beside a ditch, and crosses the line of a former railway along which the **Downs Link ◀** has been routed. Continue ahead and come to a minor road (grid ref: 194093) which leads to Botolphs. St Botolph's Church stands a short distance to the left.

Botolphs is a peaceful little hamlet with neither pub nor shop, the nearest accommodation for South Downs Way walkers being either in Bramber or Steyning. The Saxon church here glows orange towards sunset, but apart from that there is just a farm or two and a few cottages, although the village was once considerably larger and had a salt industry and fishing. But the sea withdrew from the valley of the Adur and left Botolphs literally high and dry. In the Middle Ages its fortunes drifted out with the tide, and the odd hummocks seen in some of the meadows are all that remain of one-time village houses.

STAGE 6
Botolphs to Washington

Distance	7 miles (11km)
Maps	Harvey South Downs Way 1:40,000; OS Landranger 198 Brighton & Lewes 1:50,000; OS Explorer 122 South Downs Way, Steyning to Newhaven and 121 Arundel & Pulborough 1:25,000
Accommodation	Wiston (+1½ miles), Washington
Refreshments	None on the route

Climbing out of the valley of the Adur the South Downs Way soon leads onto the Downs again with lovely intimate vistas of knuckled coombs and mounded brows. A narrow country lane is crossed near the head of Steyning Bowl, then the continuing bridleway enters a broad, inner countryside of wood-lined fields over Steyning Round Hill, where a number of Bronze Age cremation urns were discovered in 1949. Chanctonbury Ring is visited next. This crown of beech and sycamore, seen from so many different points along the Downs – and from the Weald below – that it has almost become a symbol of the South Downs, was badly hit by the storm of October 1987, and it will take decades before the recovery is complete.

When the South Downs Way was first opened, and it went no further west than Buriton, Chanctonbury Ring marked the halfway point. The remaining trees mark the site of an Iron Age hill fort and Roman temple, while a couple of miles or so to the south, Cissbury Ring is noted as being the largest and most impressive of the earthworks on the South Downs, where remains of 200-odd neolithic flint mines have been found. Cissbury, however, is not on the line of the South Downs Way – although it would be worth visiting on a future occasion. (It is in the heart of excellent walking country.)

Once again there are no refreshments available on this stage, but for those in need of a drink or a meal when Washington is reached, a pub is found in the village.

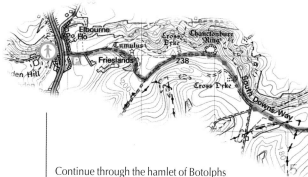

The Saxon church of St Botolph serves a tiny community on the west bank of the Adur

Continue through the hamlet of Botolphs heading away from the church for about ½ mile. The road eases uphill, curving to the right beside an attractive flint wall at Annington Old Farmhouse. Just beyond Annington House the road bends sharply to the right. Now cut off to the left along a tree-lined track, which serves as the drive to a cottage.

Just before reaching it the track forks. Bear right and climb on to gain the back of the Downs. As you gain height there is a tendency to keep peering off to the left where folding hills tuck themselves into Winding Bottom, a most attractive little vale with Coombe Head protecting it to the south. The sea lies not much more than 3 miles away, but the South Downs alignment begins to edge inland, and sea views soon recede.

The track leads to Annington Hill where a fairly straight route is followed heading south-west along the crest. On reaching a narrow hilltop road turn right through a gate and go

along the edge of a field keeping parallel with the road. At the end of the field section exit through another gate, continue beside the road for about 200 yards, then cross left to a farm track striking through a large arable field. On coming to crossing tracks note the memorial on the left, dedicated to the memory of a Sussex farmer whose ashes, along with those of his wife, were laid to rest here 'on his cherished Downs'. The left-hand track goes to Cissbury Ring and is followed by the **Monarch's Way**. ▶ The South Downs Way continues ahead.

The Way is clearly marked at all junctions, and maintains a north-westerly course among largely arable land. As you progress, so the crown of Chanctonbury Ring grows in stature ahead.

The **Monarch's Way** is a 609-mile (980km) long-distance path based on the journey taken by Charles II following defeat in the Battle of Worcester in 1651. Starting in Worcester it makes a long circuitous route and ends in Shoreham. There is a three-volume route guide written by Trevor Antill (Meridian Books).

The River Adur at Botolphs

Accommodation: About half a mile before reaching Chanctonbury Ring, a way cuts off to the right, and descends through Chalkpit Wood by way of a track. At the foot of the Downs the track joins the narrow Chanctonbury Ring Road which leads to Wiston, for those who've arranged accommodation there.

The Way continues, and rises across a green meadowland from which splendid views are to be had off to the right if you stray a little from the path. Wiston House is seen below, and a vast patchwork of fields, woodlands and meadows of the Weald stretching to the north, east and west. You may be able to detect the white-painted Shipley windmill (owned for many years by Hilaire Belloc), about 6½ miles away to the north. So come to **Chanctonbury Ring** (grid ref: 139120).

On my first walk along the South Downs Way I had looked forward to greeting the hilltop grove of beeches for some time, but feared what I might find after the ravages of the Great Storm. From afar Chanctonbury

Chanctonbury Ring was planted in 1760 by Charles Goring of Wiston House, seen below to the north-east. The grove of beech and sycamore trees was especially set to please the eye. It is said that during the first few months after planting, Goring made regular visits to his young trees, carrying water up the steep slope to ensure they 'took'. An Iron Age fort of about 4 acres forms the base of the Ring, and following the storm of 1987 the site was properly excavated before replanting took place. The Romans had built a temple in the heart of the site during the third or fourth century AD. Chanctonbury Ring is said to be haunted, and a first-hand account of this appears in Robert Macfarlane's wonderful *The Old Ways* (Hamish Hamilton/Penguin, 2012), when he recounts an experience he had when sleeping out one night in the midst of the Ring. Spooky stuff!

appeared to have survived. I had looked up from the depths of the Weald, and gazed at it from prominent positions along the eastern Downs and all had seemed well. But as I walked across the meadow towards it, the grey light of an overcast day shone on forlorn, leaning trunks, huge upturned discs of earth, and on the exposed and ruptured root systems. And my heart fell. For 200 years these trees had impressed themselves on the

Chanctonbury Ring, storm-battered, but still a major landmark on the Sussex Downs

Sussex landscape, but the winds that tore across southern England in the early hours of 16 October 1987 had effectively altered the landscape. I returned several times over the ensuing years, and noted how many of the fallen trees had been removed and young trees planted in their place. Maturity will not return overnight, but nature is incredibly patient, and no doubt our children's grandchildren will be able to enjoy what we once knew as the beech crown of Chanctonbury Ring standing proud once more. Until the next major storm, that is.

The Way skirts the Ring along its southern edge and continues heading west, but shortly after passing below a trig point, veer leftwards through a gate by a cattle grid (there is a restored dew pond on the right) and remain on the track until coming to a major junction where you turn right. Now descend a chalk and flint track, which leads to a car park a little south of Washington.

As you leave the car park bear right along a track which passes above the former main road. When it curves to the right, go ahead on what is a private drive but public footpath. Passing a few houses come to a multi-junction of tracks and cut back to the left to descend round a wooded bend and join the road. Walk along the road, then take the second turning on the left, The Street, at grid ref: 122127. (For refreshments ignore this turning and keep ahead a short distance to find the village pub beside the road. There's a campsite on the north side of the A283.)

Bypassed by the busy A24 and A283, Washington is a neat, compact village dating from Saxon times, with several attractive flint- and brick-built cottages, and a parish church with 13th-century columns and arches and a solid-looking 15th-century tower – all that remain of the previous church which was pulled down in 1866.

STAGE 7
Washington to Amberley

Distance	6 miles (9½km)
Maps	Harvey South Downs Way 1:40,000; OS Landranger 198 Brighton & Lewes and 197 Chichester & The South Downs 1:50,000; OS Explorer 121 Arundel & Pulborough 1:25,000
Accommodation	Storrington (+1¼ miles), Rackham (+1 mile), Amberley
Refreshments	None on the route, but there is a café and pub in Amberley

Between the cut made through the Downs by the valley which now carries the A24, and the twisting river valley of the Arun, the South Downs present a broad-topped escarpment of fields sown with wheat, barley or oil-seed rape, tufted here and there with trees. In places the long-distance walker or rider is rewarded with views into the depths of the Weald; sometimes over lonely farms and later, out to the glint and glimmer of the River Arun drawing itself through the low country of the north. Down there too, best seen from Rackham Banks, are the water meadows of Amberley Wild Brooks – marshlands drained by dykes and ditches, a criss-cross of watercourses picked out by the sun. Beyond the marshes and Arun's valley, the wall of the Downs slopes onward in an enticing arc.

It is another stage without habitation, although there are one or two isolated barns, and at Chantry Hill and Springhead Hill narrow lanes come onto the lip of the Downs from Storrington, whose village houses are tucked against the northern slopes. Cattle graze in large open meadows. There are hares and peewits and big skies conjuring Turner canvases on wild-weather days.

Please note, the Alternative route (formerly the Main route) makes a dangerous crossing of the A24 and cannot be recommended, but is given merely for completeness. It should only be taken on the rare occasion that there is little traffic.

Walk along The Street, and just beyond the Parish Church a road bridge crosses the A24. When the road forks soon after, branch right on a stony track/drive which leads to Rowdell House. Immediately before it bends to the right by the house, turn left on a bridleway among trees, then out to a surfaced drive passing a couple of houses, now rising as a sunken lane through woodland. Keep alert for a sign indicating the SDW breaking to the right among bushes and trees, then emerge to a sloping meadow. The Way rises across this meadow, curving left and climbing onto Barnsfarm Hill where it heads south to a crossing track used by the Alternative route (see below) at grid ref: 104119. Turn right.

Alternative route: From Washington car park bear left. Cross the A24 dual carriageway – **with great care** – and follow Glaseby Lane which winds uphill. About 200 yards from the A24 note a drinking-water supply on the left. The lane ends in woodland, and continues as a flint track rising up the slopes of Highden Hill, on the western

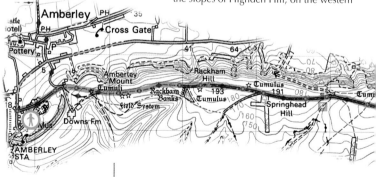

side of which it is joined by the main route of the South Downs Way coming from the right at grid ref: 104119.

Main walk continued: The Way continues towards a Dutch barn and, following a fence line across the grassland of Sullington Hill, comes at last to a small car parking area at the head of a narrow lane on Chantry Hill overlooking Storrington. This is a noted local viewpoint and a place where horses are often brought to exercise. Standing just to the right of the SDW track is the Chantry Post, similar to the Keymer Post seen near Ditchling Beacon on Stage 4.

   Accommodation: If you intend to seek accommodation in Storrington leave the Way here and travel down the lane which leads directly to the village.

I had already been walking for several hours when I arrived at the Chantry Post, so sat with my back against it to eat my sandwiches. Almost immediately the heavy clouds that had been overhanging Storrington swung away to the south-west, rose up the hillside and perched sullenly on Springhead Hill to block my advance. The air turned cool, a breeze huffed across the Downs and suddenly lightning streaked across the sky. Thunder roared and the ground shook. There was nowhere to hide, no shelter from the rain that came racing in great rods from the west, so I put my sandwiches away, pulled

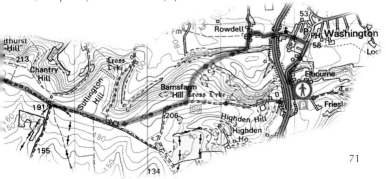

The Chantry Post is found midway between Washington and Amberley

on waterproofs and headed into the eye of the storm. A magical pathway then led between shafts of lightning (fenceposts of fire), though I saw little of the countryside to the right or left, blinkered as I was by the visor of my cagoule. Twenty minutes later the worst was over and I resumed my lunch among the puddles of a dripping spinney.

With the Chantry Post to your right continue straight ahead along a clear flint track that gently crosses a line of minor hills in a north-westerly direction. In places (so I have found since that first storm-bound journey) a view opens to the left to show the sea and the outline of the Isle of Wight far off. On meeting the head of another narrow lane on Springhead Hill, where there is also a car park, the route veers slightly left. There are hedges and clumps of trees and much arable farmland as you approach Rackham Hill.

All around Rackham Hill there are tumuli. To the south, a mile or so away and reached by a track known as the Lepers Way, is the site of a Bronze Age barrow (The Burgh), while ahead, alongside the route over Amberley Mount, there are lynchets which an archaeological survey revealed as a system of 20 fields, some of which had been terraced 2500 years ago.

Along the track by Rackham Banks you gain those splendid open views into the Weald where Parham House sprawls in its deer park backed by extensive woodland. Ahead (west) across the Arun's gap, the wooded slopes of the South Downs curve far into the distance luring you on. It is a lovely stretch to walk and, presumably, also to ride. Easy underfoot, easy on the eye; a peaceful, generous landscape. Eventually the Way leads down to a gate with the large conglomeration of barns and outbuildings of Downs Farm seen below. Go through the gate and descend the slope to pass well to

Amberley is one of the most attractive villages in Sussex

the right of the farm. An enclosed bridlepath then leads to a road where you bear right for about 80 yards. On coming to a junction where you gain a sneak view of **Amberley** turn left into High Titten (grid ref: 034125).

Amberley is one of the most attractive of all Sussex villages, and is well worth a visit. It has many charming thatched cottages, and others whose gardens cascade over their walls. Next to the Norman church stand the ruins of a 14th-century castle built for the Bishops of Chichester around a former manor house. North of the village stretch Amberley Wild Brooks ('Wild' is a derivation of 'Weald'), an area of some 30 acres of grazing marshes and water meadows spreading out from the Arun.

Mill Lane, the lane which runs between High Titten and Amberley village

Accommodation: For those needing accommodation in Amberley do not turn left here but continue ahead down the lane known as Mill Lane. This meets the B2139 at minor crossroads. Cross directly ahead into the village where there is a village store, post office, tea room and B&B.

High Titten slopes downhill between deep chalk quarries, although that on the right is mostly hidden by bushes and trees. That on the left contains **Amberley Museum** which can be seen between the trees, while sometimes you can hear the whistle of a steam engine deep below. On reaching the B2139 turn right onto a raised path running alongside the road towards Amberley. (Refreshments available at both pub and café 500 yards down the road to the left.)

Accommodation: If your plan is to stay overnight in Arundel turn left along the B2139 and follow this down to Amberley railway station – pub and café nearby. Trains run south from here to Arundel – the next station.

Amberley Museum was created from a large chalk quarry on the east bank of the Arun, which at one time employed more than 100 men. The 36-acre site has a variety of industrial machinery on display, as well as a narrow gauge railway, blacksmith's shop, clay-pipemaker's and woodturner's shops and a printing works. The museum is open to the public between May and October, Wednesday–Sunday, and daily during the school summer holidays.

STAGE 8
Amberley to Cocking

Distance	12 miles (19km)
Maps	Harvey South Downs Way 1:40,000; OS Landranger 197 Chichester & The South Downs 1:50,000; OS Explorer 121 Arundel & Pulborough and 120 Chichester 1:25,000
Accommodation	Houghton (+½ mile), Bury (+1 mile), Gumber Bothy and camping (+1 mile), Graffham (+1 mile) Heyshott (+1 mile), Cocking (+¾ mile)
Refreshments	None on the route, except water tap on the outskirts of Cocking, but pub in Houghton, 400 yards off-route near the start

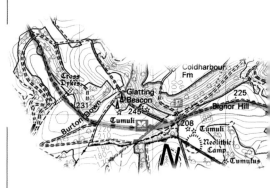

Westbound: map continues on page 83

Given private transport arrangements this lengthy stage could be broken either at Bignor Hill, or after about 6 miles at the crossing of the A285 south of

Petworth. The way to Bignor Hill conjures up visions of the Roman era, for the South Downs Way briefly shares the route of the Roman Stane Street. Burton Down gives way to more arable farmland, but west of the A285 there is much woodland and for several miles views are severely restricted. Strips of farmland break up the extensive woods, but once Manorfarm Down is reached, vistas open once more above the little village of Cocking – a village with an attractive heart and welcome prospects of refreshment and lodging.

When the path beside the B2139 runs out, cross the road with care and continue on a path now on the left of the road, behind a hedge. This brings you to a concrete farm drive where you turn left, soon to cross the railway line. Beyond a water treatment plant maintain direction on a track which twists around fields and brings you to the **River Arun**. Bear right to a bridleway bridge, provided in 1994 by the Sussex Downs Conservation Board as part of a safer alternative to the original South Downs Way route, which previously followed the busy road into Houghton.

The Arun at Amberley

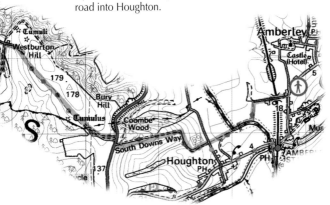

The **River Arun** is the longest in Sussex, rising in St Leonard's Forest near Crawley and discharging into the sea at Littlehampton. It is a popular river with anglers, for whom chub, pike, perch and roach are tempted. There is a very pleasant riverside walk between Amberley and Arundel, while the bankside path continues all the way to the estuary at Littlehampton. During the Napoleonic Wars a canal was built to join the Arun with the Thames via the River Wey. A wharf stood on the river then, near Houghton bridge, and chalk barges traded along the navigation. The canal was closed in 1868.

Accommodation: For accommodation in Bury, cross the bridge and turn right to follow the riverside path all the way to the village.

Cross the bridleway bridge over the Arun and bear right along the west bank. When the river curves to the right, leave the embankment to cut left on a bridleway alongside a drainage ditch. On the far side of the field turn right and soon go through a gate on the left. Continue to the Houghton–Bury road. (Accommodation and refreshments in **Houghton** 400 yards to the left.) Cross this minor road and maintain direction on a track sloping gently uphill. It snakes round to the right above a lovely little valley and, still rising, offers views of the twisting Arun below, and the village of **Bury** ◀ beside it. Now the track curves left and at the top of the slope brings you alongside Coombe Wood to reach the A29 (grid ref: 004118). Bear right for 100 yards, then follow a chalk track on the left towards Houghton Forest. From this track look back to enjoy a wonderful panoramic view which includes the Weald, Amberley Wild

Bury is a neighbour both to Houghton and Amberley, an attractive riverside village (there used to be a ferry allowing easy access to Amberley) with a secluded air about it. Novelist John Galsworthy lived in the mock-Tudor Bury House from 1926 until his death in 1933.

Houghton stands a little above the River Arun, and the South Downs Way used to go through it until a diversion took the route away from the busy road. The village has several interesting buildings, one of which is the George and Dragon, where the young Charles II supposedly stopped for refreshment in October 1651 during his flight to France following defeat in the Battle of Worcester.

Brooks, distant downland ridges, and the Arun sidling through the valley. Beside the forest the Way bears right, soon leaving the edge of the trees to cut through open fields on Bury Hill. ('To this green hill a something dreamlike clings...' said Galsworthy in his poem *Bury Hill*.)

The track becomes enclosed by fences and bordered by cowslips among the banks of Westburton Hill. Sloping downhill the Way brings you to some barns in a sunken hollow, and just beyond these there's a junction of tracks. Bear left, then immediately turn right to climb uphill alongside hedges, over crossing tracks and ahead beside a fence marking the way to Bignor Hill. To the north, at the foot of the Downs, lie the ruins of Bignor Roman Villa.

Shortly before gaining the summit of Bignor Hill, the Way passes a mounting block known as Toby's Stone – a memorial to one-time secretary of the Cowdray Hounds, Toby Wentworth-Fitzwilliam.

Once the home of novelist John Galsworthy, Bury lies across the River Arun from Amberley

The sign on Bignor Hill which shows the Roman name for Chichester (Noviomagus)

Over Bignor Hill is a car park close to the line of the Roman **Stane Street** and an interesting finger post bearing Latin names: Noviomagus (Chichester) and Londinium (London). Passing this post to your left continue ahead towards a pair of aerials. About 200 yards from the post bear left along the agger (or embankment) of Stane Street, then right at the first junction (grid ref: 970128).

Stane Street is a Saxon name for the Roman road built in AD 70 for both military and economic purposes to link Chichester (Noviomagus) with London (Londinium). It was metalled and had a camber, and was 20–25 feet (6–7.5m) wide. This remarkable piece of engineering had to cross not only the South and North Downs, but also the greensand range of hills and the almost impenetrable Wealden forest. It achieved the 56 mile (90km) route in three straight lines, including a passage through the 2000-acre estate attached to the Roman villa at Bignor. This is found below the Downs a short distance away from the point at which the South Downs Way crosses. Bignor Roman Villa is open to the public throughout the year, with the exception of Mondays between October and March.

Accommodation: If you plan to spend the night at the National Trust's Gumber Bothy (a camping barn with 25 dormitory beds plus camping, with kitchen, showers and pay phone: www. nationaltrust.org.uk/slindon-estate) do not turn right here, but continue ahead along Stane Street for ¾ mile, then veer left at a signed junction. The bothy is just 1 mile from the South Downs Way – not 1¾ miles as the Bignor Hill signpost suggests.

Having turned right, away from the route of Stane Street, in a few paces go through a gate into a field below the aerial masts, and maintain direction alongside a fence. On the far side of the field exit through another bridle gate and continue over crossing tracks. Passing a few yew trees on Burton Down the Way heads north-west across arable land (the woods on the right descend the scarp slope into the delightfully named Scotcher's Bottom), and then descends through woods on a clear track which brings you to the A285 Petworth–Chichester road at Littleton Farm (grid ref: 951144).

Coming down the track in the mid-afternoon, birds were mostly silent, but there were numerous wild flowers clustered at the base of the trees and along wayside banks to brighten the walk. Small flies danced as though riding gossamer yo-yos in misted beams of sunlight that chequered the track around me. I wandered down on stepping stones of shadow.

Cross the road and take the track opposite which passes to the right of the farm between grassy banks and trees. On coming to crossing tracks go into the field ahead (to the right of a rising track) and cross uphill through the field, veering slightly to the right in order to find another bridle gate in a mid-field fence, then continue to the upper edge of the top field.

My heart went into my mouth as a partridge leapt out of the young corn beside me, and when I recovered from the shock and looked around, I saw the pleading eyes of the hen bird gazing pitifully from her maternal egg-protecting squat. The cock had raced away to

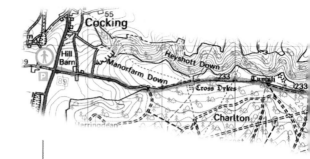

*distract my attention, leaving the hen bravely sitting
out the danger. 'Bloody daft place to lay your eggs!' I
scolded, 'the path'll be crawling with ramblers 'ere long.'
Leaving her in peace, I almost detected her sigh of relief.*

At the head of the field a broad track leads into
woodland above Stickingspit Bottom near the high
point of Crown Tegleaze (830ft/253m). This is the start
of a long section with no buildings in sight for more
than 3 miles, much of the way devoid of views. It goes
through and alongside woods over Woolavington
Down and Graffham Down, the dense woodlands
hiding deer, the seemingly endless rectangular fields
between the woods haunted by pheasants. There are
several alternative paths and tracks cutting from it, but
the route of the South Downs Way is obvious, if not
waymarked at every junction.

> **Accommodation:** At the end of a long field sec-
> tion, where the Way becomes pincered by woods
> once more on Graffham Down, a junction of tracks
> marked by an oak signpost offers one of two ways
> by which to divert to Graffham – below the Downs
> to the north (right) for overnight accommodation.

On the way through the woods on Graffham Down, note
two open sites (one on the right, the other to the left of the
track) where patches of downland are managed by the

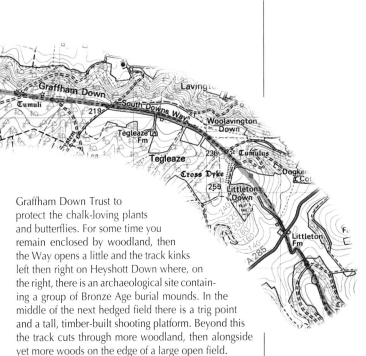

Graffham Down Trust to protect the chalk-loving plants and butterflies. For some time you remain enclosed by woodland, then the Way opens a little and the track kinks left then right on Heyshott Down where, on the right, there is an archaeological site containing a group of Bronze Age burial mounds. In the middle of the next hedged field there is a trig point and a tall, timber-built shooting platform. Beyond this the track cuts through more woodland, then alongside yet more woods on the edge of a large open field.

It was late in the day and I'd seen no-one for several hours, but I'd not been alone as there was plenty of wildlife for company. Now I spied a dog fox padding with exaggerated stealth across the field before me, head forward, back low, tail extended. The field was being picked over by innumerable pheasants, and the fox had one unsuspecting bird in its sights. Dinner was less than a minute away when, for some unknown reason, the fox glanced in my direction. He froze – as did I. Then in-built fear spun him around and, forsaking his meal (or at least, postponing it) he raced for the cover of the woods. I sensed, rather than heard, his curses. But there were no thanks from the pheasants, which continued their scrabbling undisturbed.

Eastbound: map continues on page 76

83

The flint track then descends through more open countryside as Manorfarm Down spreads itself fanshape to the west. And at last you come to the buildings of Hill Barn Farm about 250 yards before the A286 on Cocking Hill. There is a drinking-water tap on the left of the track by the entrance to a sawmill.

> **Accommodation:** To reach Cocking for accommodation, refreshments, or to stock up with supplies from the village store, bear right through the farm on a track leading down to the village, which you reach below the charming little church. Take the lane left of the church and this will bring you to the heart of Cocking by the village store, close to the Blue Bell Inn.

The Way continues beyond Hill Barn Farm and soon reaches the Midhurst–Chichester road (grid ref: 875166). There is a bus stop nearby which is useful if you plan to divert from the route to visit either Midhurst to the north, or Chichester to the south. Cocking lies ¾ mile down the road to the right.

Cocking is a small village astride the A286, but away from the road it remains remarkably unspoiled. Several of the houses in and around the village belong to the Cowdray Estate, their window frames painted custard yellow. There was a settlement here before the Norman conquest, and the Domesday Book records '…a church, 6 serfs and 5 mills yielding 37 shillings and sixpence.' The church stands on the eastern end of the village with fields around it, and is worth visiting. Manor Farm shares the churchyard wall, and below it runs a clear stream in a peaceful setting. About 3½ miles to the south at Singleton, the Weald and Downland Open Air Museum is a fascinating collection of traditional buildings in a rural setting – well worth a visit on a future occasion.

STAGE 9
Cocking to South Harting

Distance	7½ miles (12km)
Maps	Harvey South Downs Way 1:40,000; OS Landranger 197 Chichester & The South Downs 1:50,000; OS Explorer 120 Chichester 1:25,000
Accommodation	Elsted (+1 mile), East Harting (+1 mile) South Harting (+¾ mile)
Refreshments	None on the route

This stage of the South Downs Way makes a very fine journey, full of variety and interest. There are sections where the views are extensive, and others in which woodland draws a secluded landscape. There are isolated farms tucked away from the world just off the trail, with practically no other habitation and no villages of any size for many a long mile. Once again the route hugs the northern edge of the escarpment, but gazing south it is possible to catch a glimpse of Chichester's cathedral spire framed within a tree-crowded panorama. In the woods encroaching on the trail you may catch sight of deer. Certainly there will be numerous birds to serenade the day, and wild flowers in plenty.

An easy track leads onto Cocking Down, then to Linch Down, broad and open. Monkton Down leads to Philliswood and, emerging from the light glades of these woodlands, a delightful countryside is revealed. On the approach to Beacon Hill one rejoices in the landscape, and over Harting Down the northern slopes plunge to tiny communities snug in the shadow of the Downs. Rarely will you travel this last downland brow alone, for there is a car park nearby and a road that leads from Petersfield. Across this the SDW bridleway continues to a second road, the B2146, which has a path running adjacent to it down to South Harting, while the main route avoids the village and aims towards Hampshire. But this is reserved for Stage 10.

Yet again this stage is entirely without refreshment (except by diversion from the route), so set out for the day suitably provisioned.

From the A286 south of Cocking village the South Downs Way heads north-west along Middlefield Lane, passing a farm and rising towards Cocking Down. The white chalk track is enclosed by hedges at first, but on gaining the crest of the Downs bare fences replace them. Off to the left stretches an extensive area of woodland, inhabited by deer, some of which emerge at night in small herds to sleep in the wheatfields, thus flattening the crops and causing problems at harvest time.

For 3 miles the track maintains a steady north-westerly direction across Cocking Down, Linch Down (with the trig point of Linch Ball in the middle of a field to the right), and Didling Hill. On the proverbial clear day, not only Chichester Cathedral may be seen across the intervening woods, but also the Solent and the Isle

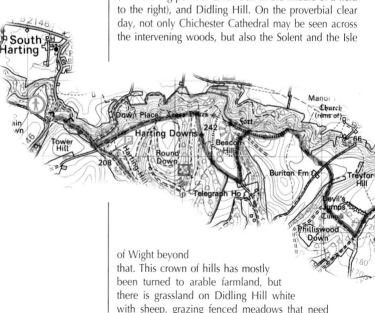

of Wight beyond that. This crown of hills has mostly been turned to arable farmland, but there is grassland on Didling Hill white with sheep, grazing fenced meadows that need no shepherd to keep watch. Then the track is absorbed into a tunnel of trees and scrub, with a high fence on the left containing the secluded, virtually unseen, Monkton House. In its grounds peacocks can be heard screeching.

One peacock had somehow escaped the lofty barrier and ran ahead of me along the muddy track, its exotic feathers dragging behind, reminding me of a bride opting for extravagant fashion in place of traditional white. Now and then it stopped to check if I was still following, then took off once more. Stupid bird, I feared I might chase it all the way to Winchester.

The track swings to the left with open meadows on the right, and by a stile a small memorial stone bears the simple inscription: 'Mark liked it here. 23.7.60–20.4.98.' Just ahead, on the edge of Philliswood, a series of curious mounds can be seen – the tumuli, or burial mounds, known as the Devil's Jumps, which date from the Bronze Age – about 3500 years ago. Philliswood Down is clothed in lovely mature beech, oak and birch trees, and the Way takes you through the woodland into a delight of birdsong in the morning, among multi-shades of green in the leaves, on the trunks and in the ground cover of sunlit glades.

Come to a crossing track and break away sharply to the right. As the Way slopes downhill it joins a broader track, eventually leaving the woods behind to gain views ahead which include the little communities of Treyford

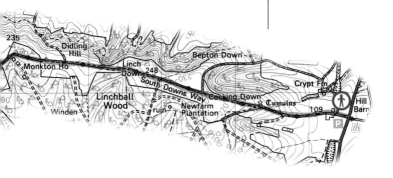

Telegraph House is partially hidden at the end of a long drive on the south slope of Beacon Hill, and was built by Earl Russell on the site of one of the Admiralty's Portsmouth to London telegraph stations established during the Napoleonic Wars. Earl Russell's brother, the philosopher Bertrand Russell, later turned the house into a (short-lived) school.

From Pen Hill, two tracks can be seen on neighbouring Beacon Hill. The SDW is the left-hand option which angles below the summit

and Elstead in the distance. Across to the left the shape of **Telegraph House** can sometimes be seen above the trees on the southern slope of Beacon Hill.

Coming to a narrow farm track (grid ref: 821178), with Buriton Farm huddled in a dip of folding hills to the left, bear left for a few paces, then turn right (there are no waymarks) through a bridle gate onto an enclosed track heading north-west once more. The Way skirts the edge of a spinney, then along the bottom edge of a field to a crossing track (grid ref: 816184).

Accommodation: If you have planned to spend the night at Elsted, bear right here. The village is about 1 mile away to the north.

Cross straight ahead, then veer left to climb the slope along a scrub-and-thorn margin between fields. This is Pen Hill, and from the crest there is a splendid panorama to enjoy.

On my most recent journey along this route rain cascaded down and created a fine mist through which no views could be seen at all. But I recalled my first wandering here, which offered a total contrast: I'd stripped off my shirt in the spring warmth, and lay for a while in the grass gazing into a hazy blue vault where half a dozen skylarks trilled with an enthusiasm impossible to check. Turning to the east my eye caught the sweeping Downs brunched with spring colours in the trees and shrubs of the northern slopes. To the west Beacon Hill, site of an Iron Age hill fort of 40 acres, was scarred with two distinct white tracks across which shadowy four-legged figures loped to and fro. Far views were distorted, but that did not matter. Nearer to hand there were flowers in the field margins and blossom among the blackthorn. I saw a rabbit break cover and nervously make a stuttering run across the bay below. Ants pioneered a new route up the face of an upturned slice of flint. A pheasant cackled, a cuckoo called, while sheep in valley meadows sent messages in the breeze. Unused to such busy peace, city folk might call it silence. It was not. In the calm hush of morning were countless sounds of life – but nothing at all with an engine. All was just as it should have been. There was undisturbed perfection in the slow revolving minutes, as I lay there and absorbed it all in solitude.

Before leaving Pen Hill, study Beacon Hill to the west and note that it is the left-hand chalk track that should be taken (although the right-hand option makes a short cut over the summit of the hill and rejoins the South Downs Way proper at Bramshott Bottom, thus saving about ¾ mile). Descend steeply into the

*South Harting lies
in the valley below
Harting Down*

saddle between Pen Hill and Beacon Hill, then fork
left to traverse round the east slope above the coomb
known as Millpond Bottom. The Way takes you along
the edge of a large field and comes to trees, scrub and
gorse bushes near the entrance to Telegraph House. At
a crossing track by the entrance, head sharply to the
right along a scrub-lined track with a rich variety of
plants growing beside it. This leads along the neat vale
of Bramshott Bottom, and comes to crossing tracks in
an open grassy saddle marked by a prominent wooden
post set on a stone base (grid ref: 803186). Turn left to
gain Harting Down – a nature reserve owned by the
National Trust, which is a popular excursion for motor-
ists who park on the western side.

To the west of Harting Down you come to a car
park and, just beyond this, cross the B2141 and continue

along a track which parallels the road among some fine mature beech, oak and chestnut trees. This pleasant stretch is known as The Bosom, and it cuts round the flank of Tower Hill to meet the B2146 above South Harting (grid ref: 783185 – accommodation, refreshments). The village is off to the right, while to the left the road leads to Uppark and, eventually, to the coast.

> **Accommodation:** If it is your intention to stay overnight in South Harting – or you need refreshment at the White Hart – do not use the road, but cross on the continuing Way, then turn right on a footpath that descends through woods and enters the village just south of the church, a distance of a little over ½ mile.

South Harting is a compact little village with a 14th-century church dedicated to St Mary and St Gabriel. Shortly before he died, the Victorian novelist Anthony Trollope lived here. The village is perhaps best known for the dignified mansion of Uppark which stands on Tower Hill to the south, at which the mother of H. G. Wells was housekeeper in the late 19th century. Uppark is in the care of the National Trust; it suffered a disastrous fire in 1989, but has since been rebuilt at great expense.

STAGE 10

South Harting to Buriton (Queen Elizabeth Forest)

Distance	3½ miles (5½km)
Maps	Harvey South Downs Way 1:40,000; OS Landranger 197 Chichester & The South Downs 1:50,000; OS Explorer 120 Chichester 1:25,000
Accommodation	Buriton (+½ mile)
Refreshments	None on the route

This short stage which leads to the outskirts of Buriton takes the route out of Sussex and into Hampshire, and marks the original completion of the South Downs Way before the extension to Winchester was approved in 1989. It is a stage in which there is a change in landscape, forgone – albeit temporarily – are the rolling Downs, and in their place a typically southern countryside of low farmland with woods and hedgerows and winding lanes. But it is no less interesting for that. There are plenty of spring and summer flowers in the hedgerows and field margins, and no shortage of wildlife. There will be jackdaws, no doubt, circling above the woods, and rabbits nose-twitching along the track. Peewits swoop over low-lying fields, and kestrels hover, head down, in search of an unsuspecting meal.

From the point where the previous stage paused above South Harting, a 2-mile hedge-lined track strikes across farmland with long views into the Weald, and reaches a farm on the Sussex–Hampshire border. A quiet country lane then takes over, before returning to a trackway at Coulters Dean Farm. At the western end of this another lane continues the route among woods on the way to Queen Elizabeth Forest, which is reached just above Buriton. Although there are no refreshment facilities along the route, Buriton (½ mile distant) has a pub which serves food.

From the B2146 above South Harting follow the clear hedge-lined track north-westward with views into the

Weald to the right. The track is known as Forty Acre Lane and it leads for nearly a mile alongside gentle farmland to a narrow metalled road, which it crosses. Maintain direction on the second half of Forty Acre Lane, near the end of which, just before reaching Sunwood Farm, you leave West Sussex behind and enter Hampshire. At Sunwood Farm come onto a quiet country road and turn left. In a few paces the road swings to the right and eases up a gentle slope beside a row of copper beech trees.

On coming to a minor junction branch right. The road then winds through Cockshott Wood, losing height among the trees. Do not be tempted by a track marked to Buriton, but remain on the road, passing **Coulters Dean Nature Reserve** ▸ on the left shortly before reaching Coulters Dean Farm, which shelters in a lonely hollow. The surfaced lane ends here, but the Way continues beyond the farm, now rising uphill and passing beneath overhead power cables to gain more Wealden views to the north, before coming down to Dean Barn and a pair of cottages. After these follow the metalled lane through Appleton's Copse and on to a T-junction (grid ref: 734198) opposite a parking area with Queen Elizabeth Forest stretching ahead.

Coulters Dean Nature Reserve is owned by the Hampshire Wildlife Trust and is a noted habitat for 11 types of orchid. Deer and badger feed there, and a number of butterflies gather on bright summer days, among them the Adonis Blue, Chalk Hill and Holly Blue.

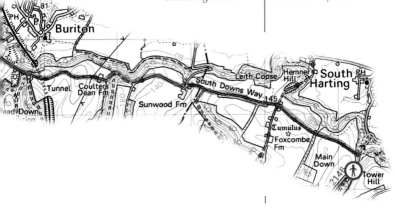

Dean Barn near Buriton

Accommodation: For those in need of accommodation or refreshment in Buriton, do not walk down the road, but take the bridleway which cuts off to the right just before reaching the T-junction.

Buriton (accommodation, refreshments) is an unspoilt village with a large duckpond, a huddle of cottages and an Elizabethan manor house behind the parish church where the historian, Edward Gibbon (1737–94) spent his early years. The village is on a bus route to Petersfield, about 3 miles to the north.

STAGE 11
Buriton to Exton

Distance	12 miles (19km)
Maps	Harvey South Downs Way 1:40,000; OS Landranger 197 Chichester & The South Downs and 185 Winchester & Basingstoke Area 1:50,000; OS Explorer 132 Winchester, New Alresford & East Meon 1:25,000
Accommodation	East Meon (+1¼ miles), Wetherdown Lodge, West Meon (+1½ miles)
Refreshments	Queen Elizabeth Country Park, Butser Hill, Meon Springs (Whitewool Farm)

On this stage of the South Downs Way there are grassy paths, broad tracks and country lanes to follow. There are stretches of dark forest with the chance of sighting deer, open hilltops with memorable, far-reaching views, tree-and-scrub-lined trackways, big fields and rolling meadows. There is

Westbound:
map continues on page 97

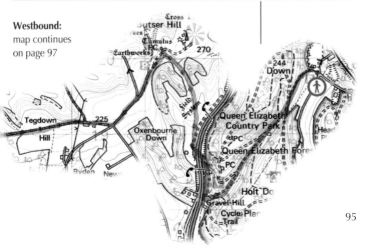

95

fast-moving traffic on the A3 (avoided by a subway), and an ancient site to wander through on Old Winchester Hill (walkers only here – the bridleway takes an alternative route). Butser Hill is the highest point, not just of Hampshire but of all the South Downs, and this is crossed in the early stages after ducking beneath the A3. After crossing Old Winchester Hill, the Way follows a delightful and rare chalk stream to the banks of the River Meon.

For those with private transport, it would be possible to arrange to break the route at the road junction of Hyden Cross.

Go through the car park and into Queen Elizabeth Forest – part of the **Queen Elizabeth Country Park** – on a broad track, which curves left as it rises along the east flank of

Queen Elizabeth Country Park (www.hants.gov.uk/countryside/qecp) consists of 1400 acres of forest and downland which includes Butser Hill. Several way-marked walks explore the woods and Downs of the park, including the 12-mile (19km) Staunton Way, a linear path, which begins here, then heads south across the Downs to Staunton Country Park, and continues alongside the Hermitage Stream to Broadmarsh on Langstone Harbour. The Hangers Way is another linear route which heads north from the park on a 21-mile (34km) journey to Alton, passing through Buriton and Selborne along the way.

hillside where one or two simple seats enjoy views down to Buriton. Over the brow of the hill ignore the first track cutting back to the right and proceed ahead until the main track forks. At this point the footpath and bridleway routes separate: the bridleway route is the left-hand track, the footpath (walker's) route takes the right branch. (The two converge later near the country park visitor centre.) On the way through the forest keep alert for

Eastbound:
map continues
on page 95

possible sightings of deer. The footpath route passes a picnic and barbecue

97

The visitor centre
in Queen Elizabeth
Country Park

area in Gravelhill Bottom, and eventually comes to a small car park at Benhams Bushes.

All was peaceful along the forest track, and as it was midweek it seemed that I had the forest to myself. Few birds sang, except far off, and my boots made little sound, and as I walked my eyes and ears were alert for wildlife. Suddenly I became aware of eyes upon me, and turning to the right-hand slope, saw a pair of deer gazing in my direction. No body markings could be seen, only heads to one side of a tree, rumps to the other. They watched me and I watched them, but their interest was less intense than mine – once they'd established I offered no threat – and growing bored with the view they vanished soundlessly into the deep security of the forest.

At Benhams Bushes come onto a narrow metalled road where you turn left to leave the forest (there is a path running parallel with the road on its left). As you exit the forest there are various small grassy areas and a number of laid-out paths. There is also a confusing super-abundance of waymarks and signs for a variety of walks and rides, which makes it necessary to study the way well. Veer right towards the park visitor centre (refreshments, public toilets). The bridleway avoids the centre itself by remaining just within the forest, but the walker's route goes right to it.

Note: There is a drinking-water tap by the path. The visitor centre and café are open daily from March to October (09.00–17.30), and November to February (09.00–16.30).

Continue beyond the visitor centre on a path above and to the right of the car park. This leads under the A3 by a subway, on the west side of which you follow blue bridleway posts bearing the SDW white acorn symbol, leading across another car park/picnic area, then through a bridle gate into an extensive grassland. Ahead rises 888ft (271m) **Butser Hill** topped by a huge telecommunications mast. Mount the steep slope of flower-starred downland, making more or less towards the mast (there

Note: For refreshments bear right through the car park to a café/toilets/information centre in a building shaped like an Iron Age roundhouse.

> **Butser Hill** is the highest point on the South Downs, the site of ancient trackways, Bronze Age burial mounds, Celtic fields and defensive dykes. There is also evidence of Romano-British occupation. On the summit of the hill stands a beacon that would have been lit in times of danger or of celebration, but this is dwarfed by the unsightly telecommunications mast. From Butser Hill a justifiably renowned panorama attracts crowds of visitors on bright summer days.

is a vague path). Near the head of the slope pause for a moment to enjoy a huge panoramic view, then go through a gate and veer left to another bridle gate near the entrance to a car park.

Bear left to Limekiln Lane which has a bridleway on its right-hand side, but which soon crosses to the left. When this eventually gives out, continue along the lane with exceptional views to enjoy, including the sea far off

From the crown of Butser Hill views extend towards Hayling Island

to the south, and the great expanse of Queen Elizabeth Forest with its straight lines of firebreaks to the west. When the lane makes a left-hand bend at a multi-way junction, take the right-hand option. Passing Homelands Farm the surfaced lane becomes a track (a true green lane), goes beneath a line of power cables and continues on an almost straight and level course across Tegdown Hill and Hyden Hill, alongside the oaks and beeches of Hyden Wood – a lovely section of ridge crest from which East Meon church can be seen off to the north-west where meadows fold neatly into a shallow valley.

Soft green shadows dappled the path. Newly unfurled beech leaves were silken to the touch and, with the afternoon light shining through them, it was possible to detect the outline fuzz of minute hairs and the rich tracery of veins within. Softly they danced up and down in the two o'clock gasp of air so that the route ahead was seen as through an ever-opening and closing Venetian blind of shadow. The next time I wandered this track I took advantage of a stile for use as a seat, and spent 20 minutes daydreaming across a meadow clotted with ewes and their lambs. Within moments they all came marching towards me from three different directions, their massed bleating announcing their expectation of something I hadn't got.

The rolling Downs below Hyden Cross near the source of the River Meon

It didn't take them long to realise I was no shepherd, and they turned away with barely a glance behind them. If they were disappointed they didn't show it, but resumed their grazing and left me in peace.

The track leads to a junction of minor roads at Hyden Cross (grid ref: 683189). The road north goes to **East Meon**, south to Clanfield and Horndean, while we maintain direction and soon come to a second junction. Go ahead up a bridleway which soon parallels a small housing development. Coming to a road, keep ahead, then take a minor road to the right towards the radio masts on Wether Down. Note that just before turning into this minor road, you pass Wetherdown Lodge on your left – an independent hostel run by the Sustainability Centre. ▶ The road becomes a track. This takes you directly past the radio masts and, on Salt Hill, the site of a long barrow in the left-hand field.

It is good to be away from buildings and on the Downs once more. Views open to the north and, although the track is confined by a fence and hedges, there is the welcome return to a sense of space. But then as you begin to slope downhill the Way becomes a sunken track on the approach to Coombe Cross. This is little more than a couple of cottages and a Georgian house on a quiet country lane (grid ref: 666210).

Accommodation: For accommodation and refreshments in East Meon, turn right and walk down the lane for about 1¼ miles.

The South Downs Way crosses the lane and continues straight ahead towards the rise of Henwood Down, but

Wetherdown Lodge is run by the award-winning Sustainability Centre (**www.sustainability-centre.org**), which, as its name suggests, is an eco-friendly organisation with a holistic approach to education through a programme of courses for adults and children. The Lodge was formerly used as accommodation for Royal Navy trainees. It has 14 rooms with 2–3 beds, and the Centre also provides overnights in tepees and yurts.

East Meon is a pretty village with the River Meon, which rises nearby, running alongside the main street. Izaak Walton, who wrote *The Compleat Angler*, stayed here to fish the local river, and one of the two village pubs is named after him. The Norman church of All Saints overlooks the village from the foot of Park Hill, its green broach spire seen from far away. The Court House is said to be of the 15th century, and there are several attractive cottages in a subtle mix of colours, some of which date from the 18th century.

about ½ mile from the road, at a crossing bridleway, turn left on a track which leads along the right-hand side of a large field and eventually comes onto a concrete farm road which you follow to its end at a minor road.

A big open country spreads before you. Fields are gold with oil-seed rape, green or yellow with corn, soft with meadows grazed by black and white Friesian cows. The Downs are rolled out as if for inspection. Henwood Down stands again to the north, the wooded rise of Old Winchester Hill is off to the west, and knowing our route leads across it, it seems odd that you now head away to the north. But those who would walk from A to B by the shortest route should have been with Caesar's troops and forget all about modern long-distance footpaths!

Turn right, passing Hall Cottages, then break away to the left at the entrance to Whitewool Farm. Note that refreshments and overnight camping are available here at the Meon Springs fishing lakes. Go down the farm drive between small lakes and skirt the handsome half-thatched outbuildings, then bear right on another concrete farm road that soon deteriorates to a rutted track. At a junction of tracks veer right and ascend the slopes of

The National Nature Reserve of Old Winchester Hill covers an area of 150 acres on the site of several Bronze Age burial barrows and an Iron Age hill fort

Whitewool Hanger, at the top of which you take a fence-enclosed bridleway heading left, parallel with a road.

Cross the road with care. On the other side turn left on another path that runs parallel with the road, and which eventually (after a further 500 yards or so) comes to a crossing flint track that carries the official South Downs Way from a lay-by for disabled people (the so-called 'Easygoing Trail' car park). The flint track is the Easygoing Trail, a level path created to give access for the less able-bodied to **Old Winchester Hill fort.** ▶ Turn right along this trail and follow it to the hill fort entrance. (At this point the SDW bridleway diverges from the walker's route. Cyclists and horseriders should follow Route A below.) Go through the gate and veer left, then take the path which cuts through the centre of this impressive Iron Age site. There are big views to enjoy too, with a distant sighting of Chichester Harbour, and the Isle of Wight out to the south-west.

Bridleway (Route A): Do not go through the field gate but take a fence-enclosed bridleway around the outer edge of the hill fort. The way then makes a sharp turn to the left and descends a steep slope. At the foot of this turn right along the top edge of a large field. It continues in the same direction until you face another large open field and a signed junction. Bear right round the field boundary, then left alongside a tree-lined hedgerow to rejoin the walker's route which you follow as far as the embankment of a disused railway now used by the Meon Valley Trail (see Route B).

Main walk continued: On coming to the earth ramparts on the western side of the fort go down the steep slope half-left (yellow with cowslips in spring) to leave the fort area, then along a fence-enclosed path beside a wood. Beyond the wood the Way is guided by a line of trees/hedgerow, then forks. Keep ahead with lovely views to Beacon Hill across the Meon Valley. A bridleway now traces the outline of large sloping fields, at the bottom of

Old Winchester Hill was the site of Bronze Age burial barrows, and an Iron Age hill fort. The outline of the fort is clearly evident and covers an area of about 14 acres. Much of the hilltop and the nearby coomb is National Nature Reserve, covering 150 acres in all, and is rich with downland flora and butterflies.

which you're led into a woodland shaw which often has a stream flowing through it. Turn left and come to the embankment of a dismantled railway which you cross and continue ahead.

> **Bridleway (Route B):** Cyclists and horseriders should remain on the route of the dismantled railway (now adopted by the Meon Valley Trail), and head left along it for a little over ½ mile. The way slopes down to a minor road, where you turn right for a few yards, then fork left into Shavards Lane. This leads to the A32 at Meonstoke (grid ref: 614206). Cross the road with care and keep ahead into Exton. Turn right along Shoe Lane, pass The Shoe pub, then turn left at a T-junction to rejoin the walker's route. When this breaks to the right just beyond the church, continue uphill along the lane as far as the parking area at Beaconhill Beeches, where the walker's route arrives at grid ref: 598227.

> **Accommodation:** If you plan to stay overnight in West Meon, turn right along the embankment and follow the one-time railway north-east for about 2 miles.

Main walk continued: When at last you leave the tree-lined, streamside path and come to a farm track, veer right, soon crossing a footbridge over the lovely River Meon. A few more paces brings you to the A32 on the outskirts of Exton (grid ref: 618213). Cross over with care and take the minor road opposite into the village, bearing right to pass the church. To the left the lane leads to the village pub, The Shoe.

Exton (accommodation, refreshments) is a pleasant village happily spared traffic from the A32 by standing a little to one side of the road. Its name suggests it was a farmstead of the East Saxons. The flint-walled parish church dates from the 13th century, and has a wooden belfry. The village pub lies just to the south among a second group of cottages.

STAGE 12

Exton to Winchester

Distance	12 miles (19km)
Maps	Harvey South Downs Way 1:40,000; OS Landranger 185 Winchester & Basingstoke 1:50,000; OS Explorer 132 Winchester, New Alresford & East Meon 1:25,000
Accommodation	The Milburys (nr Beauworth), Chilcomb and Winchester
Refreshments	The Milburys (nr Beauworth) and Winchester

This final stage of the journey from Eastbourne provides an assortment of scenic pleasures. The landscape changes pattern by the hour as you travel through it, whilst the Way itself varies between footpath, bridleway, track and quiet country lane. Winchester remains hidden from view virtually until the very last field path, but the heart of this historic city makes a worthy finish to the South Downs Way.

On departing from Exton the route heads roughly north-westward climbing sharply to the nature reserve on Beacon Hill – yet another ancient site. From there you pass the (unseen) site of a lost village, cross the route of the Wayfarer's Walk and take to a series of near-empty country roads and green lanes before coming to Gander Down. This is a big open countryside, a spacious land of mellow hills and gentle valleys, but from it another green lane takes you into and alongside woodlands as far as Cheesefoot Head. The end of the journey is near, but there is one last stretch of downland to cover before descending from the escarpment through a sunken lane leading to tiny Chilcomb, and from there across one final field and the M3, into the streets of Winchester.

The Way between Exton and Beacon Hill, a faint grass path in a green landscape

With Exton parish church on your right walk along the lane, which curves leftwards, then break away to the right along a track opposite a flint wall. The track cuts between Glebe Cottage and Bramcote House and leads to a stile next to a field gate. Over this walk directly ahead to a second stile (on the right), then cross the next field to the far left corner. Maintain direction to reach a farm track, and continue ahead, now crossing the near right-hand corner of the next field to locate a stile near a water trough.

Once again maintain direction to a woodland shaw and yet another stile, over which the path climbs steeply, then across the right-hand corner of a sloping field to a stile

Westbound:
map continues on page 109

Note: This section, as far as Beaconhill Beeches, is for walkers only. Bridleway users should follow the instructions in Stage 11 to reach that point.

106

found about 30 yards up the slope. In the final steep hillside meadow the path is sometimes rather vague on the ground, in which case the direction to make for is the top right-hand corner where a footpath signpost stands beside a stile leading to a country lane (grid ref: 603221).

Turn right along the lane for about 500 yards then, a little west of **Beacon Hill,** ▶ cross a stile in the right-hand hedge and take a path striking half-left to the far corner of the field. There you come to a parking area at Beaconhill Beeches where the bridleway and footpath routes rejoin (grid ref: 598227).

On leaving the car park area go ahead along the lane for almost 300 yards, with woodland to your right, then as the lane curves right, continue ahead along a farm track. A short distance beyond Lomer Cottage a few grassy mounds may be detected off to the left – all that remains of the village of Lomer which, though mentioned in the Domesday Book, died out in the Middle Ages. This is one of 90 such 'lost villages' of Hampshire. A little over ½ mile from the lane you come to Lomer Farm. Bear left by some barns, then turn right immediately after passing farm cottages. The Way bears left

Beacon Hill is yet another Iron Age hill fort site with hut circles and signs of agricultural workings. There is also a causewayed ditch considered even older than the hill fort – neolithic, perhaps? The summit of Beacon Hill is a National Nature Reserve with no less than 13 species of wild orchid growing there.

The SDW passes several attractive cottages in Exton

along another track which leads through arable farmland for more than ½ mile to Wind Farm, and is shared by the route of the **Wayfarer's Walk**. The track can be very muddy following wet weather.

Wind Farm stands on the edge of woodlands and with a minor road running by. Bear right to the road and then turn left along it for about ¾ mile. There is a path

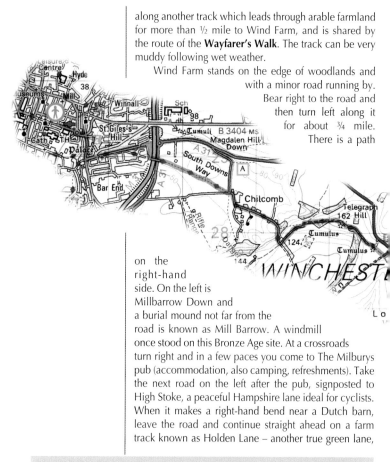

on the right-hand side. On the left is Millbarrow Down and a burial mound not far from the road is known as Mill Barrow. A windmill once stood on this Bronze Age site. At a crossroads turn right and in a few paces you come to The Milburys pub (accommodation, also camping, refreshments). Take the next road on the left after the pub, signposted to High Stoke, a peaceful Hampshire lane ideal for cyclists. When it makes a right-hand bend near a Dutch barn, leave the road and continue straight ahead on a farm track known as Holden Lane – another true green lane,

The **Wayfarer's Walk** is a 70-mile (113km) long-distance walk developed in 1981 by Hampshire County Council. It begins at Emsworth Marina and finishes at Inkpen Beacon on the Hampshire–Berkshire border, crossing on the way Walbury Camp, at 974ft (297m) the highest chalk hill in southern Britain. The South Downs Way is crossed between Lomer Farm and Wind Farm.

which leads for almost a mile through pleasant countryside, passes Holden Farm and comes to the A272 Petersfield to Winchester road (grid ref: 561269).

Cross the road with care and continue ahead on a short, tree-lined track which brings you to a field gate. Through this the bridleway bears right to follow the boundary hedge. In the first corner the bridleway route turns left with the hedge, and eventually

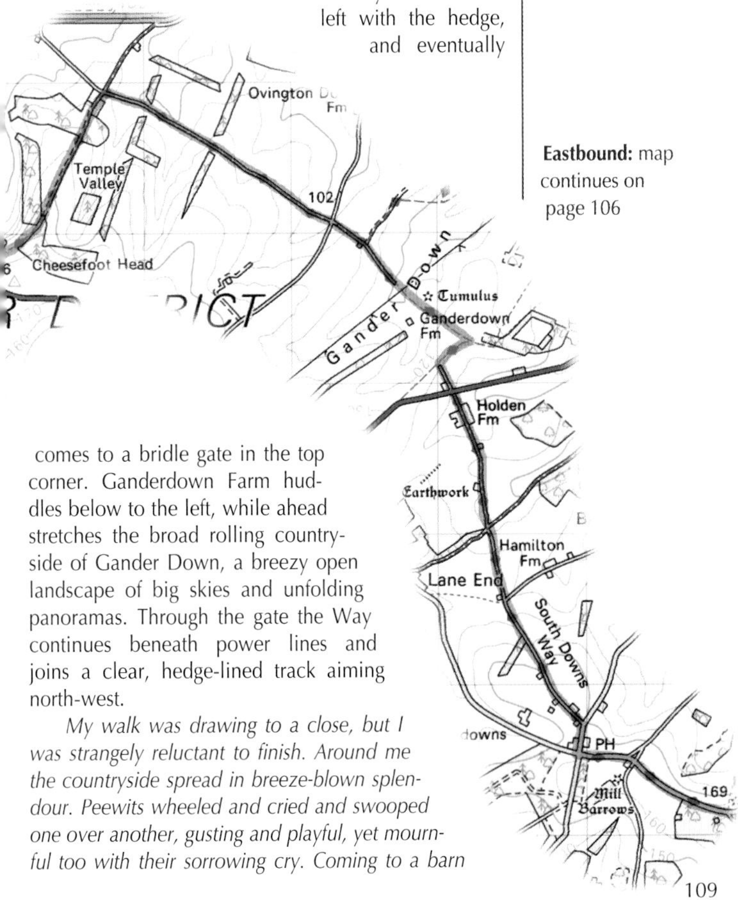

Eastbound: map continues on page 106

Ovington D Fm

Temple Valley

102

Cheesefoot Head

Gander Down

☆ Tumulus

Ganderdown Fm

Holden Fm

Earthwork

Hamilton Fm

Lane End

South Downs Way

owns

PH

Mill Barrows

169

comes to a bridle gate in the top corner. Ganderdown Farm huddles below to the left, while ahead stretches the broad rolling countryside of Gander Down, a breezy open landscape of big skies and unfolding panoramas. Through the gate the Way continues beneath power lines and joins a clear, hedge-lined track aiming north-west.

My walk was drawing to a close, but I was strangely reluctant to finish. Around me the countryside spread in breeze-blown splendour. Peewits wheeled and cried and swooped one over another, gusting and playful, yet mournful too with their sorrowing cry. Coming to a barn

109

Typical SDW marker post in Hampshire

stocked with straw bales I settled myself out of the wind to eat my sandwiches and let the miles since Eastbourne shuffle themselves in my mind. It had been a grand walk – it still was – and my love for the ever-varied landscapes of Britain had grown stronger with each succeeding day. Now I stretched out in comfort and watched a puff of raincloud sweep my way. 'Precipitation in sight', as they say on the shipping forecast. It came, dampened the track, rattled on the barn roof, and was gone again. Sunshine took over. A hare loped along the track and confronted a cock pheasant only a few feet from where I sat. They stared at each other, then carried on with their own business, totally unaware that I was watching. The cock bird then caught sight of something of interest and strutted away, head projecting like a Victorian spinster scurrying off to Mattins. Five minutes later a hen pheasant emerged from the adjacent field through an open gateway, and stood looking for her mate, squinting up and down. I was tempted to tell her where he'd gone, but decided to remain incognito and let the natural world continue around me, undisturbed by my presence. After all, who was I to interfere?

The track crosses Rodfield Lane and maintains direction for a further 1¼ miles until reaching crossing tracks at a group of farm buildings. Bear left to pass the flint-walled Keeper's Cottage (barns on the right), and continue through woods on a clear trail. Beyond the woods follow a hedge-line, then through a bridle gate to an enclosed path along a splendid avenue of beech trees with Great Clump Woods to the left. Eventually arrive beside the A272 at **Cheesefoot Head.** ◄

Cheesefoot Head east of Winchester makes a natural amphitheatre and is where General Eisenhower addressed the Allied troops in 1944 before the D-Day landings.

Across the road another bridleway leads through a field for about 100 yards to a path junction. Turn right among trees and scrub to an enclosed continuing track.

Approaching Telegraph Hill's tumulus the Way leads between a plantation on the left and a field on the right, beyond which it curves leftward and reaches a crossing track (grid ref: 517281). Turn left and follow this to Little Golders and a narrow metalled lane where you turn right to slope downhill between high banks. The lane leads to the hamlet of Chilcomb, the last habitation before Winchester. As you enter Chilcomb (accommodation) note the black-timbered grain store on staddle stones seen across a hedge on the right.

At a road junction bear right beside a flint wall. (The rather fine Saxon church of Chilcomb stands at the end of the left-hand lane.) A few yards later come to a Y-shaped road junction with a few steps leading to a gap in a hedgerow directly opposite.

> **Bridleway (Route A):** The way ahead is for walkers only. The bridleway turns right here along Kings Lane, then left on the A31. After passing under a bridge turn left up a rising bridleway which brings you onto the bridge to rejoin the footpath route. This is another 'temporary' route – watch for notices.

Main walk continued: Go through the hedgerow gap and walk alongside the very last field, with Winchester now in view ahead. On the far side of the field bear left through scrub to cross the M3 by footbridge, then swing right on the tarmac path along the outer edge of town. At an obvious T-junction of paths turn left alongside trees to reach Petersfield Road. Walk straight ahead, eventually passing All Saints Church on the left, and slope downhill, where Petersfield Road becomes East Hill and shortly after comes to a crossroads. Turn right into Chesil Street. At a roundabout bear left and cross the bridge over the River Itchen to King Alfred's statue. Continue ahead into the main shopping area, then left where signs indicate, to reach Winchester Cathedral – a fitting climax to the South Downs Way.

Winchester (accommodation, refreshments) was the Saxon capital of England, but is now very much a small city wrestling to find harmony between the old and the new. There is much of interest – historically, architecturally, spiritually. There is the famous College, founded in 1382; the Pilgrims Hall where pilgrims stayed on their way to Canterbury; the fine old City Mill (built 1774, owned by the National Trust); the lovely houses, archways, castle ruins, the Hospital of the Holy Cross. But the cathedral is the most obvious, for this is the very heart and soul of Winchester. Graceful, and at the same time, a little severe on the outside, the interior is astonishingly beautiful. Sit there at the end of the long walk and absorb the calm whispering glory that hangs in the air. The building was started in 1079 on the site of an earlier Saxon church built by King Alfred, but it was not completed until 1404, and clearly belongs to many different periods of history. Each era added something inimitable. Today Winchester is one of Europe's longest cathedrals at 556 feet (170m). But it is more than that. Enter its peaceful sanctuary and be thankful for all the days of your journey along the South Downs.

Winchester Cathedral, symbolic start or end to the South Downs Way

EASTBOUND
Winchester to Eastbourne

Beachy Head lighthouse

STAGE 1
Winchester to Exton

Distance	12 miles (19km)
Maps	Harvey South Downs Way 1:40,000; OS Landranger 185 Winchester & Basingstoke 1:50,000; OS Explorer 132 Winchester, New Alresford & East Meon 1:25,000
Accommodation	Winchester, Chilcomb, The Milburys (nr Beauworth) and Exton
Refreshments	Winchester, The Milburys (nr Beauworth) and Exton

See map on page 108

Although the long walk begins in the heart of Winchester, it does not take long to escape this small historic city in order to explore the open spaces for which the Downs are noted. Immediately after leaving Chilcomb the Way climbs onto the Downs, then follows a series of farm tracks across a rolling landscape with a surprisingly remote feel to it. Although several country roads are crossed, Exton is the only true village – and that only a small one – on this stage of the walk. However, even Exton is by-passed by cyclists and horseriders following the bridleway alternative which, in this instance, skirts Beacon Hill, loops round to Warnford (north of Exton, on the way to West Meon) and continues along a country lane heading south-east before being reunited with the walker's route near Old Winchester Hill.

On a practical level, this first stage is fairly undemanding. It's well-signed and waymarked, and the views are especially rewarding near Beacon Hill and Old Winchester Hill.

The history of **Winchester** dates back to 450 BC when Celtic tribes settled on the east bank of the River Itchen on what is now known as St Catherine's Hill. Five hundred years later (in AD 70) the Romans arrived and began to create a walled city, naming it Venta Belgarum, then with the crowning of King Alfred in AD 871, Winchester became the capital of Saxon England. (Alfred's burial site was discovered at Hyde Abbey in 1999.) Following the Norman invasion of 1066, the town surrendered to William the Conqueror who built himself both a palace and a castle, and 20 years later the Domesday Book was compiled here.

From **Winchester** Cathedral make your way to the eastern end of the High Street known as Broadway. This is where you'll find the town's bus station, tourist information (in the Guildhall), and an impressive statue of King Alfred the Great.

Leaving Alfred's statue and the cathedral behind you, make your way eastwards along Broadway, cross the bridge over the River Itchen (note the City Mill on the left, and turn right into Chesil Street. On reaching the far end of a car park turn left into East Hill, which forks after about 100 yards. Take the right branch along Petersfield Road, and keep on to its far end, then continue on a tarmac path along an avenue of trees. The path forks by the first South Downs Way sign. Bear right, and very soon you'll cross a bridge over the M3, on the far side of which the way forks once more.

Bridleway (Route A): At this point the bridleway route briefly leaves that of the walker. Cyclists and horseriders should turn right and descend to the A31 which parallels the M3. Go north for a short distance (the M3 to your left) to a roundabout, then turn right, and right again down King's Lane to rejoin the walker's footpath route in Chilcomb.

Main walk continued: Walkers turn left immediately after crossing the M3 bridge, and a few paces later enter a large field. The Way leads down the left-hand edge, with views of the wood-crowned Downs running in a

This old barn, perched on staddle stones, stands in a garden beside the SDW in Chilcomb

long line ahead. At the far side of the field go through a gap in the hedgerow onto a junction of lanes on the edge of Chilcomb (accommodation, public telephone), a small but attractive village of farms and pleasant houses. Here walkers are reunited with the bridleway route.

Go ahead on the lane signed to St Andrew's Church, soon passing a fine thatched barn at the entrance to Manor Farm. When the lane forks by a flint wall, bear left (the right branch goes to the Saxon church of St Andrew), and after passing a few houses note the black timber barn standing on staddle stones in the garden of one of the last buildings on the left.

The narrow lane rises between tree-lined banks and ends at the start of a track by a house named Little Golders. Turn left along the track until it kinks on an open crown of a hill at a junction, from where you gain a last view of Winchester, and turn right along a grass track between a fence and a hedge. Keep along the right-hand field boundary as it skirts just below the wooded top of Telegraph Hill, and on reaching a four-way crossing, bear left across a field to the A272 at **Cheesefoot Head** (there's a car park to the right). ▶

Cross the road directly ahead onto a narrow fenced path. This leads along the edge of Great Clump beech-wood, with the slope plunging steeply to the left. Beyond the woods continue on a farm track that eventually takes you past the flint-walled Keeper's Cottage. About 100 yards beyond the cottage, turn right on another track (King's Way) which now leads for 1¼ miles between fields to Rodfield Lane.

Maintain direction on the continuing track across Gander Down. There's a junction of tracks by a Dutch barn where you keep ahead with rolling country spread all around. The Way takes you into a meadow where you pass well to the left of the black barns of Ganderdown Farm. Follow the left-hand boundary of a second meadow and, shortly before reaching its top left corner, cut across to the boundary half-right ahead and turn right. Having made a dog-leg turn, keep the hedge on your left (Holden Farm is seen below) and soon come to a field gate and a stile on your left. Through the gate walk down a farm track to the A272 Petersfield to Winchester road (grid ref: 561269).

Cross the road with care and, passing Holden Farm on your left, continue ahead on the track known as Holden Lane through pleasant country-side for almost a mile, before joining a very narrow metalled lane (Westfield Drove) by another Dutch barn. Keep ahead, passing a few houses, and come to a T-junction by Windmill Cottage. Turn right, and a short way along the road pass The Milburys pub (accommo-dation, also camping, refreshments). At the crossroads a few paces later, turn left (sign to West Meon).

A short distance along the road you gain a fine view to the north. On the right there's a Bronze Age burial mound shown as Mill Barrows on the map. When the road forks continue ahead, now with a bridleway running along its left-hand side. This eventually regains the road opposite a track near the entrance to Wind Farm. Follow the track/stony drive towards the farm, then continue alongside a

Cheesefoot Head is where General Eisenhower addressed the Allied troops in the early summer of 1944 before the D-Day landings.

The **Wayfarer's Walk** was developed by Hampshire County Council and opened in 1981. It stretches for about 70 miles (113km) between Emsworth Marina and Inkpen Beacon on the Hampshire–Berkshire border, and is waymarked. See *Along and Around the Wayfarer's Walk* by Linda Herbst (Hampshire County Council).

little woodland, then on the left-hand edge of a large field on a path shared by the **Wayfarer's Walk**.

On coming to the first buildings of Lomer Farm, turn right then left and, immediately past a barn complex, turn right again onto a stony track. This takes you past the site of one-time Lomer village which died out in the Middle Ages (one of numerous 'lost villages' of Hampshire). Lomer Pond is half-hidden among trees on the left and, shortly after passing this you come onto a country lane along which you walk ahead to where it bends sharply to the right at Beaconhill Beeches, where there's a car park (grid ref: 598227). Cyclists and horse riders leave the main SDW here and follow the lane down to Exton.

The walker's footpath route takes the right-hand of two field gates ahead, then scores through the centre

The 13th-century church in Exton stands beside the South Downs Way

Head-high cow parsley flanks the path on Beacon Hill above Exton, where views stretch to the Isle of Wight

of a field with **Beacon Hill** ▶ on the left. A stile in the opposite boundary delivers you onto a narrow metalled lane where you turn left, soon gaining splendid views into a deep coombe on the right. About 500 yards down the lane cross a stile on the left into a steeply sloping meadow overlooking the Meon Valley. Descend into the valley by stiles linking a series of fields, with occasional yellow disc markers to direct the way.

Eventually enter Exton (accommodation, refreshments, public telephone) and turn left along a narrow road passing attractive houses and the church of St Peter and St Paul. At a junction just beyond the church, note that the village pub, The Shoe, is on the right-hand road, Shoe Lane.

Exton is a charming small village with the little River Meon sidling through. The name suggests it originated as a farmstead of the East Saxons; the church is 13th-century. Accommodation may be found here, and also in neighbouring Corhampton, Meonstoke and Droxford.

Beacon Hill
is a National Nature Reserve on an Iron Age hill fort site, on which there are said to be more than 13 varieties of orchid growing.

STAGE 2
Exton to Buriton

Distance	12½ miles (20km)
Maps	Harvey South Downs Way 1:40,000; OS Landranger 185 Winchester & Basingstoke and 197 Chichester & The South Downs 1:50,000; OS Explorer 119 Meon Valley and 120 Chichester 1:25,000
Accommodation	East Meon (+1¼ miles), Wetherdown Lodge (nr East Meon), Buriton (+¼ mile)
Refreshments	Meon Springs (Whitewool Farm), Butser Hill, Queen Elizabeth Country Park, and Buriton

See map
on page 96

Several high points on this stage make it a particularly memorable one. The National Nature Reserve of Old Winchester Hill is one – an elevated Bronze Age site with far-reaching views, visited soon after leaving Exton. Salt Hill near Mercury Park to the south of East Meon is another, as is the lovely trackway across Highden and Tegdown Hills on the way to Butser Hill. Butser Hill is the highest point on the South Downs Way with a panoramic view to catch your breath. Then, a little above Buriton, there's the Queen Elizabeth Forest in which there's a possibility of sighting deer. Although Buriton lies just off the route of the South Downs Way, it is well worth a diversion – whether you plan to spend the night there or not.

River Meon This delightful chalk stream is the main river of south-east Hampshire, and its source is a series of springs in a coombe below where the SDW crosses Hyden Hill. It gives character to a number of quintessential Hampshire villages (East Meon is the first and loveliest), and gained fame for its trout fishing thanks to Izaak Walton's classic book *The Compleat Angler*.

The River Meon, a lovely chalk stream, at Exton

Leaving Exton, curve left alongside a flint wall and come to the A32. Cross it with care aiming half-left to a small track which leads to a footbridge over the **River Meon**. A path now curves towards Shavards Farm, then decides better of it, crosses a track and goes along the left-hand edge of a field before plunging along a narrow woodland shaw. During, or following wet weather, a stream runs through this shaw.

Coming to a brick bridge on a dismantled railway, either go beneath the arch or, if the stream is flowing, cross the embankment and descend the other side on steps. You then cross to the right-hand side of the shaw where waymarks direct you out of the trees and back alongside a wire fence.

Following fences the route, a bridleway, curves round the edge of fields and climbs a slope towards Old Winchester Hill. Pause during the ascent to enjoy good views back to Beacon Hill across the valley. Just below the upper west slope of Old Winchester Hill the route divides. The footpath route goes along the left-hand side of a line of trees/hedgerow, while a bridleway keeps to the right-hand side.

Note: This first section is for walkers only. Horseriders and cyclists should follow the directions given on the next page.

121

Whitewool Farm in its valley below Old Winchester Hill

Old Winchester Hill is a National Nature Reserve covering 150 acres in all, with earthworks of an Iron Age hill fort and Bronze Age burial barrows.

Coming to the nature reserve of **Old Winchester Hill** ◀ the footpath ascends a scrub-covered slope, then through a gate up the right-hand side of the hilltop crown among masses of **cowslips** in springtime. A trig point marks the top of the hill, and from it you can enjoy a spectacular 360-degree panorama. In this view the Isle of Wight can be seen to the south.

Over the summit bear left on a crossing path which leads to a seat and an information board. Go through a gate to the right of these, and walk ahead – there are two parallel routes, both of which lead to a gate and a road. Do not go onto the road, but turn left along the SDW bridleway running parallel with it. Maintain direction until a signpost directs you across the road, through a gap in a hedge, and along a fence-enclosed bridleway at the top edge of a meadow. This brings you to a point close to a road junction.

Cowslips are symbolic of the Downs, and these lovely yellow-headed plants will be seen in abundance along the route in April and May. The name originates from the belief that the flower would appear wherever there was a cowpat! For centuries it was used as an ingredient in the manufacture of vinegar, mead, wine and even cheese.

Bridleway route: In Exton proceed along Shoe Lane to pass The Shoe pub, shortly after which you bear left. On coming to the A32 cross with care and keep ahead along Shavards Lane. When this forks take the right branch, and after a few yards leave the road for a signed bridleway on the left. This rises onto the embankment of a disused railway, which you now follow for a little over ½ mile until coming to a SDW signpost directing you to the right.

The way enters a field which it skirts to the right, then turns left between a fence and a hedge. Rising steadily towards the wooded Old Winchester Hill, after ¾ mile the way veers to the right along the top boundary of a large field. On coming to a signed junction, branch left below Old Winchester Hill's steep slope and after two more fields come to another SDW signpost. Turn sharp left and climb the steep slope between fences. At the head of the slope the way turns right along the outer edge of the hill fort, to rejoin the walker's alternative SDW route as described.

Go through a bridle gate on the right and cut back in a dog-leg to angle downhill through a sloping meadow with Whitewool Farm seen in the valley below. At first the Way is faint, but it soon becomes a more profound track which eventually cuts left and takes you directly to Whitewool Farm.

Pass round the left-hand side of the farm, then over a charming stream (part of the Meon Springs Fly Fishery; refreshments, camping) to a T-junction of narrow roads. Turn right along a peaceful valley scene, with radio masts directly ahead on distant Wether Down. About 150 yards beyond Hall Cottages turn left up a concrete farm road between fields, rising across the slope of Henwood Down. Continue ahead when the concrete ends. The spire of East Meon church can be seen, but as you descend into a dip, it disappears completely. At a crossing path turn right – unless, that is, you have arranged accommodation in **East Meon**.

With the River Meon flowing through, East Meon lies just over a mile off the South Downs Way

East Meon is a pretty village with the River Meon flowing through it. The Norman church of All Saints overlooks the village from the foot of Park Hill (splendid view from the hill), it has a green broach spire and, inside, a black marble font brought from Belgium in the 12th century. The Court House nearby dates from the 15th century and is where the Bishops of Winchester used to hold court. East Meon, and the neighbouring hamlet of Frogmore, contains many attractive cottages in a subtle mix of colours, although a number were lost when a fire raged through the village in 1910. Among those destroyed were two low thatched cottages that served as the local workhouse.

Accommodation: For accommodation and/or refreshment, keep ahead along the track which leads to a country lane where you bear left and soon enter East Meon. This is one of the loveliest of villages near the route of the South Downs Way. It has two pubs, a B&B, shop, post office, public telephone and bus services to Southampton, Winchester and Petersfield.

The continuing South Downs Way goes between hedges and trees and spills out to a country road at Coombe

Cross. Maintain direction on a bridleway that rises between trees and low banks over which there are fine views to be had. A long steady ascent leads onto Salt Hill (more big views) and Wether Down with its tall radio masts. Keep ahead on a stony track which goes alongside the boundary fence of the former HMS *Mercury*, now known as Mercury Park. Note that on your right you pass Wetherdown Lodge, an independent hostel run by the Sustainability Centre. ▶

Turn left at a crossing road and follow the bridleway that runs parallel with it on the right-hand side. This eventually brings you down to a junction of roads. Keep ahead to a second road junction at Hyden Cross (grid ref: 683189), and maintain direction, now on a track beside Hyden Wood and across Hyden Hill and Tegdown Hill. When the woodland ends, note there's a path on the left (not part of the SDW) which descends to the source of the River Meon and, about 2 miles from here, to East Meon.

The continuing track becomes a surfaced drive which leads to a three-way junction of narrow roads. Bear left towards a large radio mast on Butser Hill.

Wetherdown Lodge is run by the Sustainability Centre (**www. sustainability-centre. org**), an eco-friendly organisation that runs a programme of courses for adults and children. Formerly used as accommodation for Royal Navy trainees, the Lodge has 14 rooms with 2–3 beds, and the Centre also provides overnights in tepees and yurts. An on-site café is open daily (10.00–16.00).

East Meon is glimpsed from Hyden Cross

The Queen Elizabeth Country Park sign on Butser Hill

Note: For refreshments, continue ahead through the country park car park to a kiosk housed in a replica Iron Age roundhouse (also toilets, information, picnic tables and a panoramic view). The refreshment kiosk is open 10–5.30 – weather depending – at weekends and in school holidays.

Before long you'll find an enclosed bridleway running along the right-hand side of the road. It then crosses to the left-hand side for about 100 yards, to the entrance to **Queen Elizabeth Country Park** on Butser Hill (refreshments). ◀

The SDW crosses the road again and follows a path which skirts the top edge of a scrub slope below the refreshment kiosk, then goes through a bridle gate onto well-cropped downland. Bear half-right towards a second gate, and through this a faint grass path continues slightly left ahead. Halfway down the slope pass through a third gate beyond which the gradient steepens before easing at the lower part of the slope. In the bottom left-hand corner come onto a clear fenced path with a barbecue area to your right. It leads through a car park, across the approach road, then on a path heading right to pass through a tunnel beneath the A3.

Just before reaching the country park visitor centre the Way divides. Left through woods for the bridleway route, straight ahead for walkers. The walker's route passes behind the visitor centre (refreshments) and alongside a picnic area, and continues to a car park entrance

Queen Elizabeth Country Park is jointly managed by Hampshire County Council and Forest Enterprise. Covering some 1400 acres (564 hectares), it is dominated by the open dome of Butser Hill, and on the east side of the A3, by the wooded Holt Down and War Down which are covered by the Queen Elizabeth Forest. A large section of the country park is designated as a National Nature Reserve, boasting 38 species of butterfly and 12 species of wild orchid. (For more information visit www.hants.gov.uk/countryside/qecp.)

where you bear half-left across a road, then left on a path shared by the **Hangers Way**. ▶ This very pleasant woodland path takes you behind and beyond a small parking bay, and shortly after it forks. Veer left onto the service road near a hairpin bend, and walk ahead through the Benham Beeches parking area onto a stony track which rises steadily, and near the head of the slope is joined by another from the right – the bridleway route.

Keep ahead, ignoring the left branch when the track forks soon after. Before long the Way curves to the right and descends to Halls Hill car park where you leave the Queen Elizabeth Country Park at a three-way road junction (grid ref: 734198), just ½ mile from Buriton.

Accommodation: If you're in need of refreshment or accommodation in Buriton, do not walk down the road (signed to the north) but take the bridleway which heads into woods just across the road junction. This makes a delightful approach to the village.

Buriton (accommodation, refreshments) is an attractive, unspoilt village with a large duckpond near the church. The 18th-century historian, Edward Gibbon, spent his early years in the Georgian manor house which stands nearby. Until 1989 Buriton marked the western end of the South Downs Way. It has a pub, B&B, post office/village store next to The Five Bells, public telephone and buses to Petersfield.

The **Hangers Way** is a 21-mile linear route which heads north from the Queen Elizabeth Country Park, passes through Buriton and Selborne, and ends in Alton. It briefly shares the route of the SDW through Queen Elizabeth Forest.

STAGE 3

Buriton to South Harting

Distance	3½ miles (5½km)
Maps	Harvey South Downs Way 1:40,000; OS Landranger 197 Chichester & The South Downs 1:50,000; OS Explorer 120 Chichester 1:25,000
Accommodation	South Harting (+½ mile)
Refreshments	None on the route

See map
on page 92

On this short stage the route makes a transition from rolling downland to an agricultural landscape typical of the southern counties, with hedge-lined fields and meadows dotted with farms. There are still distant views to enjoy, and the Downs are never far away, but this low-lying countryside has a different quality to that through which the walk has journeyed thus far. Despite this difference, the route remains full of variety and natural beauty.

After a short spell along a quiet country lane above Buriton, the Way then follows an undulating trackway as far as Coulters Dean Farm where another lane – banked with wild flowers in springtime – curls below the hills. This leads to a large farm and a long hedge-lined track that takes the South Downs Way out of Hampshire and into West Sussex. At the end of this track, known as Forty Acre Lane, the Downs are regained once more above the village of South Harting.

At the road junction above Buriton take the narrow lane signed to Dean Barn. This ends after about ½ mile at a pair of cottages where a trackway continues, soon affording a view north to Petersfield. Shortly after passing beneath power lines you come to Coulters Dean Farm and the start of another country lane.

Buriton lies just below the SDW. When the route first opened, the village marked the western extent of the Way

The trackway known as Forty Acre Lane near South Harting

Coulters Dean Nature Reserve has been owned by the Hampshire Wildlife Trust since 1996. It is the habitat of deer, badger and various species of butterfly. As many as 11 types of orchid are also found there.

On the right stretches the woodland of **Coulters Dean Nature Reserve,** ◄ and the lane winds below it, the wayside banks bright with wood anemone, violet, wild garlic and primrose in spring. For about ¾ mile keep to the lane as far as Sunwood Farm. Here you curve sharply to the left, then leave the lane and take a stony hedge-lined track on the right, rising between fields. When it forks take the left branch sloping downhill a little to cross the unmarked boundary between Hampshire and West Sussex at a point known as Hundred Acres. The countryside spreads out to the north where the Weald provides contrast to the wooded Downs that rise a short distance to the south.

After almost a mile the track comes to a very narrow lane by a house named Downlands, from which you can see directly ahead to a ruined tower (a folly) on Tower Hill above South Harting. Keep ahead, now on the track known as Forty Acre Lane, which leads to the B2146. On the approach to this road South Harting comes into view below, the green copper spire of the church directing your attention. Just before you come to the road a footpath breaks away to the left as a direct route to South Harting, for those in need of accommodation or refreshment.

South Harting (accommodation, refreshments) lies just ½ mile off the route of the South Downs Way. It has B&B, a shop, post office, pub and public telephone, and buses to Chichester and Petersfield. It's a compact village with a 14th-century church whose unusual dedication is to St Mary and St Gabriel. Shortly before he died, the Victorian novelist Anthony Trollope lived here, but perhaps South Harting is best-known for the dignified mansion of Uppark which stands on the upper slopes of Tower Hill to the south. Built in the late 17th century, the house became home for a while to the young Emma Hart who was brought here by Sir Harry Fetherstonhaugh – before she became the second Lady Hamilton and Nelson's mistress. A century later the housekeeper at Uppark was Mrs Wells, mother of H. G. Wells who described life below stairs in his *Experiment in Autobiography*. The great house passed into the hands of the National Trust, who largely rebuilt it after a disastrous fire in 1989. It is open to the public.

STAGE 4
South Harting to Cocking

Distance	7½ miles (12 km)
Maps	Harvey South Downs Way 1:40,000; OS Landranger 197 Chichester & The South Downs 1:50,000; OS Explorer 120 Chichester 1:25,000
Accommodation	East Harting (+1 mile), Elsted (+1 mile), Cocking (+½ mile)
Refreshments	None on the route

See map
on page 86

The Downs are regained above South Harting, and once again large panoramic views reward much of the way, especially from Harting Downs and Pen Hill. Woodland crowds the route in places, but open spaces are the norm on this stage where the South Downs Way tends to hug the northern edge of the escarpment.

*Marker post
between Beacon Hill
and Harting Downs*

Cross the B2146 at grid ref: 783185, and take a pleasant woodland path which curves above a second road (the B2141) among mature beech, oak and chestnut trees on the slopes of Tower Hill. When the path comes to the B2141 cross with care and enter the National Trust-owned Harting Downs Nature Reserve.

Passing through a belt of trees you then cross a slope of open downland below a car park, with extensive views over the Weald. A clear chalk path crosses the Downs just below the head of the slope, with a wonderful panorama spreading far to the north, east and west. When the path briefly fades, marker posts conveniently guide the way until an obvious chalk track appears, sloping downhill between scrub hedges into a grassy 'saddle' that effectively separates Harting Downs and **Beacon Hill.** ▶

Beacon Hill was developed as an Iron Age fort around 300–200 BC. Although the SDW skirts below its summit, paths lead onto the crown at 794ft (242m), which makes a splendid vantage point.

Accommodation: If you've arranged accommodation in East Harting bear left here and descend directly to the village.

Ignoring a path which climbs the steep slope of Beacon Hill, a cairn-like marker directs the Way to the right, angling gently across the flank of the hill above the dry valley of Bramshott Bottom.

At the head of the slope go through a bridle gate and soon after turn sharp left in a wooded corner near **Telegraph House**. Heading north along the east slope of Beacon Hill above Millpond Bottom, views open once more, with conifer-fringed Pen Hill seen as the next obstacle to be crossed by the SDW.

Turning east away from Beacon Hill the Way descends to the head of Millpond Bottom and a junction of paths. Go ahead up the slope and pass over Pen Hill

Telegraph House is partially hidden at the end of a long drive on the south slope of Beacon Hill. It was built by Earl Russell on the site of one of the Admiralty's Portsmouth to London telegraph stations established during the Napoleonic Wars, and was later briefly turned into a school by Earl Russell's brother, the philosopher Bertrand Russell.

Cowslips on Pen Hill

where the view now extends beyond Treyford Hill to the long wall of the Downs fading blue with distance. The remains of Buriton Farm can be seen in the valley below to the south-east as the Way goes down the slope to a woodland corner and another path junction.

Accommodation: For Elsted turn left on a path which descends the slope and heads across fields to the village.

Turn right along the lower edge of a long sloping field, and continue ahead at the next junction, eventually leaving the field edge to twist among trees, then ahead along a fence-enclosed path.

On coming to a narrow track that leads to Buriton Farm, turn left for a few paces, then right on another track which soon angles up the south-west flank of Treyford Hill. When the track forks take the left branch. Shortly after the Way curves left and passes through woodland on Philliswood Down. On coming to a four-way junction of tracks turn left. At first the Way is flanked by scrub, then it enters woodland once more.

When the woods on the left of the track end, note the prominent grassy mounds of the Devil's Jumps

(Bronze Age burial mounds, or tumuli) in the meadow, and shortly after there's a stile and a small memorial stone inscribed 'Mark liked it here'.

The track is drawn through a tunnel of trees with the boundary of Monkton House on the right. Peacocks roam in the grounds and their tuneless cry grates by contrast with the songs of woodland birds. Then you emerge to open sheep-grazed meadows where the Way is led by wire fences across Didling Hill, Linch Ball and Cocking Down, with long views extending both north and south. When conditions are favourable Chichester, the Solent and even the Isle of Wight may be seen.

After Cocking Down and a four-way junction, the track slopes downhill and joins the very narrow Middlefield Lane, which is hemmed in by steep banks. Then pass a large dairy farm, whose houses have the custard yellow window frames of the Cowdray Estate. Beyond the farm you reach the A286 Midhurst to Chichester road at grid ref: 875166. There's a small car park on the right and bus stops nearby. It's possible to catch a bus here for Midhurst (north) or Chichester (south). Cocking lies a little over ½ mile down the road to the left, but should you need either accommodation or refreshment there, it would be safer and more pleasant to approach by a bridleway which leaves the South Downs Way by Hill Barn – see Stage 5 for details.

Cocking (accommodation, refreshments) stands astride the A286. It's a small village with B&B, a pub, tearooms, shop, public telephone and buses to Midhurst and Chichester. Before the Norman conquest there was a settlement here and the Domesday Book records: '…a church, 6 serfs and 5 mills yielding 37 shillings and sixpence.' Below and to the east of the main road, the 11th-century church is worth visiting. It stands above reedy ponds fed by Costers Brook, while Manor Farm shares the churchyard wall in a pleasant rural setting. About 3½ miles to the south at Singleton, the Weald and Downland Open Air Museum is a fascinating collection of traditional buildings and is recommended for a future visit.

STAGE 5
Cocking to Amberley

Distance	12 miles (19km)
Maps	Harvey South Downs Way 1:40,000; OS Landranger 197 Chichester & The South Downs 1:50,000; OS Explorer 120 Chichester, and 121 Arundel & Pulborough 1:25,000
Accommodation	Heyshott (+1 mile), Graffham (+1 mile), Gumber Bothy and camping (+1 mile), Bury (+1 mile), Houghton (+½ mile), Houghton Bridge (+½ mile), Amberley
Refreshments	None on the route, but water tap near start at Cocking, and café in Amberley

See map
on page 82

The early stages of this stage are dominated by woodland and views are restricted, but after crossing the A285 below Littleton Down, more open countryside draws you on across Sutton Down and Burton Down. Approaching Bignor Hill the South Downs Way briefly follows the Roman road of Stane Street, and from the crown of Bignor Hill a vast panorama opens out, with the waters of Amberley Wild Brooks and the River Arun gleaming below the blue-stretched line of the continuing Downs.

Above Cocking cross the A286 with caution and progress along Hillbarn Lane to Hill Barn Farm where you'll find a drinking-water supply on the right.

Accommodation: If you plan to visit Cocking for accommodation, refreshment or supplies from the village shop, turn left here and follow a clear track down to Cocking church. Bear left on the lane below the church; this brings you into the heart of the village by the post office/shop, and almost opposite the Blue Bell Inn.

The Way continues beyond Hill Barn as a partly-met-alled farm road, which soon gives way to a track leading between fields onto Manorfarm Down. The fields are either given over to grazing dairy herds, or to raising cereal crops. The track forks on the edge of a conifer plantation. Ignore the right branch and maintain direction, now losing views as woodland begins to crowd the way. Conifers give way to coppiced woodland at the start of Charlton Forest, and although there are several crossing tracks, the South Downs Way keeps ahead and is clearly signed. One or two redundant timber-built shooting towers are passed – apparently these were constructed by the Cowdray Estate to enable paying guests to shoot deer.

The track makes a kink left and right along the edge of a strip of meadow on Heyshott Down, where you'll see a number of Bronze Age burial mounds dating from about 1500 BC. The Way is then blinkered by woodland, and although views are concealed, the walking is easy except after prolonged rain when the track becomes very muddy.

On Graffham Down several small enclosed meadows have been set aside as part of a conservation project managed by the Graffham Down Trust to protect chalk-loving plants and butterflies.

Immediately after major crossing tracks, the woodland cuts back on the left as you come to a long three-sided field, and views are hinted once more into the Weald. Other fields stretch ahead as the Way keeps to the right-hand edge. Eventually reach another major crossing track at Crown Tegleaze, with fine views and a large fingerpost indicating East Dean to the right (south-west), and Duncton to the left. The SDW continues ahead through a brief woodland interlude, then emerges to a large open field through which you descend, passing through a second field, then down a tree-lined track to

Note: At a major junction of tracks marked by an oak signpost, the left-hand bridleway descends to Graffham in 1 mile.

Littleton Farm and the A285 Petworth–Chichester road (grid ref: 951144).

On the other side of the road a farm track winds up the slope towards Sutton Down. On the edge of woodland the track forks and you take the right branch, which takes you alongside, then through, a patch of woodland before coming onto the crown of Sutton Down. From here the best views are to the north-west, with the SDW clearly defined through the fields above Littleton Farm.

Drawing level with the trig point on Sutton Down the way forks again. Once more take the right branch ahead, and before long you reach a four-way junction on the edge of the Slindon Estate, which is owned by the National Trust.

From the Downs above Littleton Farm, Sutton Down can be clearly seen to the east

Accommodation: Gumber Bothy Camping Barn, run by the National Trust, is about 1 mile to the south-west, and may be reached by turning right at this junction. It is open from March to October (Tel: 01243 814484).

A bridle gate gives access to a meadow where you continue ahead alongside a wire fence, with big views across woodland to the coast. Leave the meadow at its far side and come onto a flint track which is part of the old Roman road of **Stane Street**, used on this stage by the **Monarch's Way**, one of the longest of all long-distance walks. (Gumber Bothy is easily reached by turning right here.) Veer left when the track forks, and at a T-junction turn right to reach the Bignor Hill car park. A large wooden signpost shows the way to Noviomagus (Chichester) and Bignor.

On Sutton Down the South Downs Way slices between large arable fields

Stane Street is the name given by the Saxons to the great Roman road which ran from Chichester (Noviomagus) to London (Londinium). Building this road must have been a considerable task, for it not only had to climb over the South Downs, it then had to contend with the notoriously sticky clay of the Weald, and the dual obstacles of the greensand hills and North Downs. The 56-mile route was achieved in three straight sections, and completed in about AD 70.

The **Monarch's Way** is an epic route of 609 miles (980km), based on the journey made by Charles II in 1651 following his escape from the Battle of Worcester. Beginning in Worcester it visits Stratford-upon-Avon, the Cotswolds and Mendips, and is met on the South Downs Way as it heads towards Shoreham-by-Sea in East Sussex. A three volume guide to the route has been written by Trevor Antill and is published by Meridian Books.

Cross the car park's approach road and take the clear track which scores through large open fields to gain the summit of **Bignor Hill**, a marvellous vantage point from which to examine the continuing line of the South Downs, as well as the snaking River Arun and the water courses of Amberley Wild Brooks. Just beyond the summit of the hill the SDW passes Toby's Stone – a memorial to Toby Wentworth-Fitzwilliam, one-time secretary of the Cowdray Hounds.

Bignor Hill overlooks the Weald with the small village of Bignor directly below to the north. This whole area resonates with Roman history, for apart from construction of Stane Street to convey goods and personnel between Chichester and London, the Romans had a large villa, presumably built for a wealthy and important official, sited a little east of where Bignor village stands today. Dating from the fourth century AD, the villa was at the heart of a large farm of about 1900 acres, it had under-floor heating and some of the finest mosaics yet discovered in England.

The descending track curves right and forks. The SDW curves left round a hairpin bend and descends past a large barn below Westburton Hill. The Way now angles up the slope among banks smothered with cowslips in springtime, and continues across large open fields to reach the A29 on Bury Hill (grid ref: 004119).

Turn right for about 100 yards, then cross the road with care onto a descending track alongside Coombe Wood, with a fine view to Houghton and the low-lying fields and meadows at the foot of the Downs. When the wood ends, the Way cuts through a large field to a narrow lane at grid ref: 017118.

Houghton stands astride the B2139 above the River Arun, and until 1994 when the bridleway bridge over the Arun was erected, it used to be on the route of the SDW. The village has several interesting buildings, including the George and Dragon in which it is said the young Charles II stopped for refreshment in October 1651, during his flight to France following his defeat at the Battle of Worcester.

Bury stands on the west bank of the River Arun opposite Amberley, with whom it used to share a ferry. This is another small and attractive village and one-time home of novelist John Galsworthy, who lived in Bury House from 1926 until his death in 1933.

Accommodation: For accommodation and/or refreshments in **Houghton**, turn right for about 400 yards. For **Bury** ▶ (accommodation, refreshments) turn left for a little under a mile.

Across the lane go ahead to a drainage channel forming a field boundary, then turn right and left along the next field boundary to gain a raised embankment above the **River Arun**. Follow this round to a bridleway bridge, cross to the left bank and turn right for about 150 yards.

The **River Arun** is the longest in Sussex, and tidal where the South Downs Way briefly meets it. During the Middle Ages the river was navigable as far as Amberley, and the castle was built during the Hundred Years' War to defend it. During the Napoleonic Wars a canal was built to link the Arun with the Thames via the River Wey as part of a scheme to connect London with the English Channel, but this was short-lived and the canal closed in 1868. Today both banks near Amberley have footpath access, while it's possible to follow the right bank path all the way to the coast at Littlehampton.

Accommodation: For accommodation and/or refreshments at Houghton Bridge continue along the riverside path.

The continuing South Downs Way turns left away from the river at a signpost onto an enclosed track that winds past farm buildings and a water treatment plant, crosses the railway line and provides a view north to Amberley Castle, before coming to the B2139 New Barn Road on

Drainage channel on the SDW near Amberley

the outskirts of Amberley (grid ref: 028124). For accommodation and refreshments, turn left.

Amberley (accommodation, refreshments) is one of the most attractive of Sussex villages with many charming thatched cottages, and others whose gardens cascade over their walls. Overlooking the marshlands and water meadows of Amberley Wild Brooks ('Wild' being a derivation of 'Weald') are the Norman church and ruins of a castle built for the Bishops of Chichester in 1380. The walls enclose a manor house that is now a hotel (www.amberleycastle.co.uk).

STAGE 6
Amberley to Washington

Distance	6 miles (9½km)
Maps	Harvey South Downs Way 1:40,000; OS Landranger 197 Chichester & The South Downs, and 198 Brighton & Lewes 1:50,000; OS Explorer 121 Arundel & Pulborough 1:25,000
Accommodation	Rackham (+1 mile), Storrington (+1¼ miles), Washington
Refreshments	Pub in Washington

See map
on page 70

Once Amberley has been left behind there's no habitation on this stage, for the route climbs onto the Downs and remains there until forced to descend to Washington in its 'dry valley'. Throughout, the South Downs present a broad-backed escarpment, fringed here and there with trees, but often with open sheep- (or cattle-) grazed grassland, or vast fields sown with cereal crops or oil-seed rape. In two places the crest of the Downs is reached by narrow roads that end in car parks (at Springhead Hill and the Chantry Post by Sullington Hill), and at weekends and holiday periods one should expect company – which comes as a shock after experiencing so many otherwise 'empty' miles along the South Downs Way. For the remainder of this stage of the route, company is more likely to be in the form of skylarks, peewits and the occasional hare. Apart from sheep and cows, that is.

Turn right on a hedge-enclosed bridleway alongside the B2139, but before long you're directed across the road where you continue on a raised path behind another hedge as far as a minor road named High Titten, where a sign indicates the midway point between Winchester and Eastbourne. (Previously the halfway point was advertised on Bury Hill west of Amberley!)

Note: There's a trough and water supply outside a café near Amberley railway station, a short distance further along the B2139.

Amberley Museum has been developed within a large disused chalk quarry that once employed more than 100 men. The 36-acre site has various items of industrial machinery on display, as well as a narrow gauge railway, blacksmith's shop and a printing works.

Turn left up High Titten and, as you ascend the slope, note views to the right into the chalk pits **museum**. ◄ Approaching the head of the slope another road cuts left to Amberley, while we turn right to pass the entrance to a large house (Highdown), and shortly after leave the road for a bridleway that rises through a belt of trees on the left. The Way then continues beside a wire fence that leads onto Amberley Mount from where you gain a splendid panoramic view that can be enjoyed all the way to Rackham Hill. Between Amberley Mount and Rackham Hill you cross an old earthwork known as Rackham Banks.

Accommodation: Shortly before reaching the trig point on Rackham Hill you meet a crossing path. If you've arranged accommodation in Rackham village, turn left and descend the steep scarp slope to the B2139 where you turn left, then right along Rackham Street.

Between Rackham Hill and Springhead Hill you briefly pass through a small woodland, then gain a view of the Channel to the south.

Accommodation: From the car park on Springhead Hill there's a path onto Kithurst Hill, with another that breaks away to descend to Storrington where there's B&B, pubs, shops – including cycle spares – post office, and public telephone.

The SDW passes to the right of the car park to cross a shoulder of Kithurst Hill, passes the first **dew pond** seen along the way, and then comes to a second car park by the Chantry Post (grid ref: 087119).

Walk through the car park and continue across Sullington Hill, which is part downland, part arable, but with a great sense of space and a trilling of larks. On reaching a solitary barn, the Way curves slightly left, and on Barnsfarm Hill you come to a finger post to be faced with two options.

Dew Ponds are found alongside the route in many parts of the Sussex Downs. By virtue of the permeable nature of chalk, there is practically no surface water on the Downs, so saucer-shaped scoops were traditionally dug out and lined with clay to trap and store rainwater for grazing animals. A number of these were later given a concrete base. Originally these ponds were known as 'cloud ponds', 'mist ponds' or, more prosaically, 'sheep ponds'.

Main route avoiding A24: One mile ahead the original SDW crossed the busy A24. Though hazardous, this option is still available (see Alternative route below), while a better and safer diversion has been created. For this turn left at the finger post and head north across Barnsfarm Hill. On the far side descend the grass slope and curve right at the bottom of a meadow, then branch left into some trees to join a narrow surfaced track. This becomes a sunken lane descending through woodland, out of which you pass a couple of houses, walk ahead among more trees, then turn right on a crossing track by Rowdell House. This track becomes a lane which crosses

The parish church in Washington

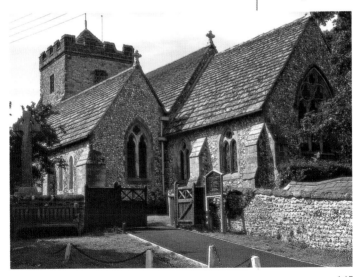

a bridge over the A24 and enters Washington (accommodation, refreshments). Passing the church walk down The Street to a T-junction where you turn right (left for the pub). Shortly before the road reaches the A24, turn left into a car park at the foot of the Downs at grid ref: 120120.

Alternative route: Be warned: this alternative section crosses the busy dual carriageway of the A24. Continue ahead from the finger post junction, with the woodland crown of Chanctonbury Hill seen a little over 2 miles to the east, and the sea at Worthing to the south. Crossing Highden Hill the way is guided between wire fences and a small woodland as you descend to the head of a narrow metalled road.

As you descend the road note the drinking-water tap on the right, opposite a bungalow. Soon after you come to the A24, which you cross with great care. On the east side turn left then right along a feeder road, and into a car park at grid ref: 120120. Washington (accommodation, refreshments) lies about ½ mile to the north, along the feeder road.

Washington is a compact village with a number of attractive flint, timber and brick-built cottages, and a parish church with a 15th-century tower, and 13th-century arches and columns that remain after substantial rebuilding took place in the 19th century. Washington grew from a Saxon settlement named for the sons of Wassa, it has a pub, B&B, bus links with Worthing, and a campsite a little to the north.

Note: A path cuts left here, which eventually leads to the A24 bridge.

STAGE 7
Washington to Botolphs (Adur Valley)

Distance	7 miles (11km)
Maps	Harvey South Downs Way 1:40,000; OS Landranger 198 Brighton & Lewes 1:50,000; OS Explorer 121 Arundel & Pulborough and 122 South Downs Way, Steyning to Newhaven 1:25,000
Accommodation	Wiston (+1½ miles), Steyning (+½–1½ miles), Bramber (+1½ miles)
Refreshments	None on the route, but a water supply at the end of this stage

See map on page 64

Climbing out of Washington's 'dry valley' the crest of the South Downs is regained at Chanctonbury Hill, with the acclaimed beechwood crown of Chanctonbury Ring nearby. Seen from the Weald far to the north, as well as from many vantage points along the SDW, Chanctonbury Ring was badly damaged by the great storm of October 1987, and it will take several decades before the programme of replanting restores it to its former glory. However, the trees mark the site of a Roman temple and an Iron Age fort, while a couple of miles or so to the south, Cissbury Ring is the largest and most impressive earthworks to be found on the South Downs. Later, the route takes you near Steyning Round Hill where a number of Bronze Age cremation urns were discovered in 1949 – proof indeed, that history is all around you on the South Downs Way.

From Washington car park south of the village, go up the track which climbs the slope between banks, winding steadily uphill to a T-junction of tracks where you turn left. The Way passes a dew pond (above and to the left of the track) on Chanctonbury Hill from where there's

Chanctonbury Ring was planted in 1760 by Charles Goring of Wiston House, an Elizabethan mansion at the foot of the Downs. The original grove of beech and sycamore trees was, and still is, a major landmark on the South Downs escarpment, and during the first few months after planting, it is said that Goring made regular visits to his young trees, carrying water up the steep slope along Wiston Bostal to ensure they 'took'. The grove is planted within the mounds of a 4-acre Iron Age earthwork that was properly excavated following the great storm of October 1987, when it was discovered that the Romans had built a temple there during the fourth or fifth centuries AD.

a magnificent 360-degree panoramic view. You then continue alongside **Chanctonbury Ring** before making a long arc to the right. At a four-way crossing track, the right branch goes to **Cissbury Ring**, while the left-hand option descends through woodland to Wiston (accommodation) about 1½ miles from here.

Cissbury Ring is the largest and most impressive of all the earthworks on the South Downs. Covering no less than 65 acres, the Iron Age hill fort that dates from about 300 to 59 BC has two clearly defined ramparts whose construction led to some 60,000 tons of chalk being removed from the intervening ditch. Long before the hill fort was begun, Cissbury had been mined for flint, with shafts up to 40 feet (12m) deep, making it one of the major sites of flint mining in southern England.

The Way continues ahead, scoring across the wide open crest of the Downs and, after another 1½ miles, comes to a second major four-way crossing at grid ref: 162100. The right-hand option also leads to Cissbury Ring, and has been adopted by the Monarch's Way, while the left-hand route offers a way down to Steyning (accommodation, refreshments, shop, bank and bus services) in about 1½ miles. Far ahead a high-rise building can be seen in Brighton, while on the right of the track note the memorial to a Sussex farmer whose ashes, along with those of his wife, were 'laid to rest on his cherished Downs.'

One of several water supplies beside the Way in Sussex – useful alike for horses, walkers and riders

The SDW maintains direction and soon joins a minor road where you walk along its left-hand side as far as the entrance to a very narrow farm road. Keep ahead through a bridle gate and then along the right-hand edge of a field. At the far boundary go through another bridle gate, then turn left down the edge of a large meadow with a view through the coombe of Steyning Bowl. The Way eventually veers away from the fence to gain another gate midway across the far boundary. This takes you down the right-hand edge of the next field, from where you have a clear view of the radio masts on Truleigh Hill to the north-east, the lovely old church of Botolphs in the valley below, with the jarring sight of a cement works chimney nearby, and south to the massive grey chapel of **Lancing College**.

Lancing College as seen from the South Downs Way is a huge grey ecclesiastical building, a classic of Victorian Gothic architecture. The chapel, for that is what dominates, was designed in the 1840s by R. H. Carpenter, whose father created the adjacent school buildings. Standing high above the town, the college looks out across the Adur's valley and Shoreham harbour towards Brighton, and was founded in 1848 with the aim of creating 'the union of classes by a common system of education' based on Christian principles.

149

Botolphs is a peaceful little hamlet with neither pub nor shop, but just a few farms and attractive cottages, and a Saxon church, dedicated to St Botolph, whose walls glow orange at sunset. The village was once much larger, with fishing and salt industries, but the sea withdrew from the valley of the Adur, leaving Botolphs literally high and dry. Odd hummocks in some of the meadows are all that remain of one-time village houses.

The **Downs Link** is a recreational route which, as its name suggests, links the South and North Downs Ways between Botolphs and St Martha's Hill near Guildford in Surrey. Established in 1984 it follows for much of its 34-mile (55km) route the course of a dismantled railway.

The final descent to **Botolphs** takes you down a tree-lined track that spills out onto a minor country road. Bear right to pass some very attractive flint-walled houses. Immediately after the entrance to Pear Tree Cottage, take the fence-enclosed bridleway on the left of the road. This leads to a lay-by and a bridleway running away from the road alongside a ditch. Within a few paces this crosses the line of a disused railway, and the start/finish to the **Downs Link**. ◄

Go onto an embankment above the River Adur, cross a bridge to the east bank and, just before coming to the A283 Shoreham Road, you'll find a water tap and trough on the right. An enclosed bridleway now takes you below the road to a lay-by/parking area near a bus stop for Shoreham, at grid ref: 197096.

STAGE 8

Botolphs to Pyecombe

Distance	7½ miles (12km)
Maps	Harvey South Downs Way 1:40,000; OS Landranger 198 Brighton & Lewes 1:50,000; OS Explorer 122 South Downs Way, Steyning to Newhaven 1:25,000
Accommodation	Truleigh Hill Youth Hostel, Edburton (+½ mile), Poynings (+¾ mile), Pyecombe
Refreshments	Devil's Dyke, Saddlescombe and Pyecombe

See map
on page 60

This stage of the Way falls into two distinct parts. The first climbs out of the valley of the River Adur and keeps to the top of the Downs along the Fulking escarpment, then descends beside the Devil's Dyke to Saddlescombe, which is little more than a farm and a group of buildings set in a saddle (or pass) within a coombe. The second part is much shorter, for it quickly regains the Downs above Saddlescombe, crosses West Hill, then slopes down to the A23 at Pyecombe, a two-part village divided in the 17th century by the plague.

Cross the A283 and turn left. Just beyond a bus stop turn right and ascend the slope of Beeding Hill through the centre of a large field. At the top of the field go through a gate and alongside the boundary fence of a meadow, then onto a narrow road next to a car park. Keep ahead, using a thin bridleway on the left of the road which takes you almost as far as Truleigh Hill Youth Hostel (accommodation, refreshments) at grid ref: 221106. A water supply is found outside the building near its entrance.

The essential Downs
above Botolphs

Remain on the stony track that replaced the met-alled road, and pass a few houses and masts to your left before coming to a large radio mast by some barns. The track passes these, then slopes downhill curving left from where the continuing SDW can be seen crossing Edburton Hill to the north-east. The way forks at the start of the National Trust's Fulking escarpment, and those who have arranged accommodation in Edburton should take the left branch. The main track veers right and pro-vides lovely views from the escarpment into the Weald.

Between Edburton Hill and Perching Hill there's a dip into a little saddle beneath a line of power cables. On Perching Hill you're on the edge of the escarpment with a long view to the north-east where downland spurs push into the Weald and Fulking village can be seen below.

Fulking Hill is next, with yet another big view which includes the Devil's Dyke Hotel half-hidden among trees. Passing through a gate on the eastern edge of National Trust land on Fulking Hill, the path forks and you take the upper, right-hand option and cross a narrow road which serves the Devil's Dyke Hotel (refreshments).

The **Devil's Dyke** is Britain's largest single coombe of chalk karst; a steep dry valley which covers 183 acres of downland. Dotted with scrub, the chalk grassland is the habitat of several orchids as well as wild thyme, horseshoe vetch and birdsfoot trefoil. The summit of the Dyke was the site of a massive Iron Age hill fort, and the whole area is now in the care of the National Trust.

Coming onto Summer Down, which is part of the Devil's Dyke Estate, keep ahead among islands of scrub, with the hollow of the **Devil's Dyke** to your left. After crossing a more open section beyond the initial scrub, take the left branch when the path forks, and you'll come to the corner boundary of an underground reservoir, then descend to a road at **Saddlescombe**.

Saddlescombe has been farmed for more than 700 years and came into the ownership of the Knights Templar in the 13th century. In 1995 Saddlescombe Farm was acquired by the National Trust. In addition to 500 acres of agricultural land, it has several unspoilt Sussex farm buildings, including a blacksmith's forge complete with furnace and bellows. There is a campsite and the Hiker's Rest café (closed on Wednesdays), which provides welcome refreshments. See www.nationaltrust.org.uk/saddlescombe-farm-and-newtimber-hill.

The view along the Fulking escarpment, near the Devil's Dyke, stretches far into the Sussex Weald

> **Accommodation:** If you have arranged accommo-
> dation in Poynings take the left-hand path running
> parallel with the road. This leads directly to the
> village.

Cross the road onto the drive leading to Saddlescombe
Farm (refreshments), then up a short bridleway which
curves right, passes behind a barn and comes onto a farm
road near a water supply. Continue past a few houses
and barns, then go through a gate to a sunken bridleway
which rises through a tunnel of trees, emerging onto the
open slopes of West Hill. Crossing the hill you gain a
view onto Pyecombe and its valley sliced by the busy
A23 London to Brighton road.

Descend to a driveway by a riding school, and bear
left alongside the A23 on a minor road which brings you
onto a bridge by which you cross the A23. On the far side
a finger post directs you along Church Hill in Pyecombe
(accommodation, refreshments). Along this lane you soon
reach the parish church at grid ref: 292126.

Pyecombe is wedged between the A23 and A273, a
small village that was badly hit by the plague in 1603,
during which some of the villagers resettled ½ mile to
the north-west. The original eastern half has an interesting church and an attractive old forge by its entrance.
The Norman church was largely built in 1170, but its
tower was added a century later. Inside there's a finely
decorated lead font, thought to have been disguised with
whitewash during the Civil War of 1645 to prevent the
lead being used to make bullets. The tapsel gate leading
into the churchyard has a shepherd's crook as a latch.
Such crooks were made for around 200 years in the old
forge nearby, not only for South Downs shepherds, but
more decoratively to be carried by Church of England
bishops as a symbolic pastoral staff. The Forge is now
a tearoom, open at bank holidays and weekends (or by
appointment for walking groups Tel: 01273 842272).

STAGE 9

Pyecombe to Housedean (A27)

Distance	8½ miles (13½km)
Maps	Harvey South Downs Way 1:40,000; OS Landranger 198 Brighton & Lewes 1:50,000; OS Explorer 122 South Downs Way, Steyning to Newhaven 1:25,000
Accommodation	Clayton (+½ mile), Keymer (+1½ miles), Ditchling (+1¾ miles), Streat (+1¾ miles), Plumpton (+¾ mile), Lewes (+1½–2 miles)
Refreshments	None on the route

See map
on page 54

Broad panoramic views are commonplace on this stage of the South Downs Way, for a large part of the route journeys along the scarp edge so you gain the perspective of height and depth as well as one of distance. The agricultural pattern that has become familiar by now, is repeated with a mixture of grazed downland and arable fields, interspersed with patches of woodland. But there's variety in that pattern, and the route is enlivened by a close view of the twin Clayton Windmills not long after setting out. Soon after, the Way crosses Ditchling Beacon. At 813 feet (248m) this is the highest point in Sussex, whose popular downland is protected as a nature reserve. Below the Beacon in Ditchling village the Romans had a fortified camp, and on Plumpton Plain there was the site of a Bronze Age settlement, while the route later skirts Mount Harry above Lewes, where Simon de Montfort took arms against Henry III in 1264. Once again, history is a frequent companion along the South Downs Way.

East of Pyecombe church, Church Hill leads into School Lane and eases down to the A273 where you turn left along a hedge-enclosed bridleway as far as a point opposite the entrance to Pyecombe Golf Club. Cross the road and follow the drive up a slope then, passing the clubhouse to your right, continue up a track that runs alongside the golf course. At the top of the slope you gain a view of the **Clayton Windmills** to the north.

The **Clayton Windmills**, known as Jack and Jill, are a much-loved feature of the South Downs. The upper, black-painted smock mill (Jack), was built in 1866 and has been converted to a private residence, while Jill, the gleaming white post mill, is in the care of a preservation society and is open to the public most Sundays (14.00–17.00) between May and September, with a tearoom providing refreshments. Jill was built in 1821 and originally stood in Patcham, Brighton, but was towed by oxen to her present site where she continued working until 1906. For further information see www.jillwindmill.org.uk.

Eventually go through a gate, and a few paces later turn left at crossing tracks and pass between the buildings of New Barn Farm. Maintain direction along the farm track towards the Clayton Windmills, but on coming to a crossing track, turn right away from them.

Accommodation: To reach Clayton village for accommodation and refreshments, turn left, then take the path which leads round the first windmill (Jack), passes the second (Jill), then descends to Underhill Lane in Clayton.

The SDW track now works its way south-east and soon reaches the Keymer Post – a fine oak post set back a little to the left on the boundary between East and West Sussex.

Accommodation: By the post an alternative path descends the steep scarp slope to Keymer for overnight accommodation.

Maintain direction along the scarp edge track, and shortly pass the gorse-fringed Burnt House Pond, with another muddy little hollow just beyond it.

With its car park nearby, **Ditchling Beacon** ▶ will rarely be enjoyed in solitude, but from the trig point on the summit the views are far-reaching. Through the car park (there's often an ice cream van) cross the narrow road with care and pass to the left of another restored dew pond.

Accommodation: For accommodation and/or refreshments in Ditchling, turn left on the road for about 50 yards where you'll find a path which soon plunges down the steep slope among trees. Maintain direction at the foot of the slope as far as Underhill Lane. Bear left, then turn right into Nye Lane after 100 yards. When this forks, take the left branch into the village. Ditchling has B&Bs, pub, post office, shop and buses.

The SDW now takes you over Home Brow and Western Brow before descending into a little dip through which a very narrow metalled lane leads to Streathill Farm.

Accommodation: For accommodation in Streat, turn left and follow the lane down to the foot of the

Ditchling Beacon is the highest of the South Downs in Sussex and is owned by the National Trust, but its nature reserve, with several varieties of orchid, is in the care of the Sussex Wildlife Trust. Marked by a trig point the summit of the hill is surrounded by the rectangular outline of an Iron Age hill fort.

Home Brow, to the east of Ditchling Beacon

Note: Refreshments are sometimes available at Streat Hill on Sundays and Bank Holidays, 9.30–17.00 – look for signs.

slope. Turn left along B2116 for about 150 yards, then right along Streat Lane.

Cross the narrow lane onto Plumpton Plain where you gain views to Plumpton, Plumpton Place, the race-course, and extensive buildings of an agricultural college below.

Accommodation: At the first junction, the left-hand option is the one to take if you require accommodation and/or refreshments in Plumpton.

A little over a mile from the narrow lane near Streathill Farm, the SDW makes a sharp right turn by a gate near the National Trust downland of Blackcap. The bridle-way is now enclosed by thorn hedges, and soon takes you alongside a small woodland, then along the edge of a large field. After about 100 yards between fences, you come to a track and turn half-left down the right-hand edge of another field, soon passing beneath power cables.

The Way continues through gates and more open fields on Balmer Down, passing another shallow dew pond. Then, at the bottom field boundary, go through a gate on the right to a narrow enclosed bridleway descending to a dip near a small electricity substation, then twisting steeply uphill through the woods of Bunkershill Plantation. Leave the woods by a bridle gate, go ahead, then down a steeply sloping field that drains into a valley cut by the A27 west of Lewes. At the foot of the slope go through another gate and turn right alongside the flint-walled boundary of Housedean Farm (grid ref: 369092).

Accommodation: If accommodation is needed in Lewes, turn left along the A27 to a bus stop for a frequent service into town. Lewes has all main services, including rail links with London.

STAGE 10
Housedean (A27) to Southease

Distance	6 miles (9½km)
Maps	Harvey South Downs Way 1:40,000; OS Landranger 198 Brighton & Lewes 1:50,000; OS Explorer 122 South Downs Way, Steyning to Newhaven 1:25,000
Accommodation	Kingston (+½ mile), Telscombe (+1¼ miles), Rodmell (+½ mile), Southease
Refreshments	Southease

See map on page 48

Between Housedean Farm and Mill Hill near Rodmell there's no habitation on the route, but instead there's a wonderful sense of space with many splendid vantage points from which to contemplate the extent and diversity of the South Downs. This short stage of the route is full of natural beauty as the Way approaches the valley of the River Ouse. The Channel is glimpsed to the south, an inner lining to the Downs to the north, and from the scarp edge there's a series of deep coombes, or dry valleys, to break the escarpment's broad smooth crest.

West of the entrance to Housedean Farm go up a minor road to cross a bridge over the A27, then slope down to the left. When the road swings round to join the A27, go ahead through a gate and along a bridleway below a railway embankment, then through an archway to the south side of the railway. The Way now goes between a field and a wooded bank, before rising through the trees to a long slope that takes you up towards the beechwood of Newmarket Plantation near the head of Cold Coombes, a fine sheep-grazed dry valley. Keeping the beechwood to your right, reach the top of the field, go through a gate and along the edge of Cold Coombes. A second gate

Juggs Road is the name given to a one-time trading route across the South Downs used by fisher-folk from Brighton, who carted their fish by donkey to the market in the county town. The people of Lewes referred to these traders as 'Juggs', supposedly from the earthenware jugs, or pots, in which the fish were salted and kept fresh.

leads the Way onto the crest of the Downs where you swing left and in a few more paces come onto a track known as **Juggs Road**. Veer left and continue alongside a fence. Reaching gorse bushes and a dew pond, which lies near the unmarked site of long-removed Ashcombe Windmill, the Way curves to the right.

Accommodation: An alternative path breaks away here to descend north-eastwards to Kingston where there's B&B accommodation.

Soon after passing the dew pond you pass a second one on Kingston Hill. This is just left of the route and is screened by more gorse bushes. Beyond it you eventually come to an obvious track stretching ahead, with the scarp slope plunging steeply to the small village of Iford, and with Lewes clearly seen to the north-east. Another track (Breach Road) descends to Swanborough Manor, while a steep and narrow coombe falls towards Iford.

Dew ponds are common on the Sussex Downs. This one lies beside Juggs Road above Kingston-near-Lewes

Keep along the track as it edges the scarp slope with an ever-evolving series of big views to enjoy.

When the track makes a sudden bend to descend as Dencher Road (not shown as such on the 1:50,000 map), continue straight ahead for about 150 yards, then go through a gate on the right and soon join a concrete farm road on Iford Hill. Turn left and follow this road, which is almost dead straight, for a little over a mile on Front Hill between open fields.

On reaching a T-junction leave the concrete and go ahead through a bridle gate, then along the edge of more fields of cereal crops or oil-seed rape, to an enclosed bridleway that almost becomes a tunnel of trees. This leads to the entrance to Mill Hill, a large house that exploits a splendid view.

Accommodation: If you plan to find accommodation in **Rodmell** turn left and walk down the drive, which leads directly to the village.

Rodmell is an unassuming village known for being the home of writers Leonard and Virginia Woolf of the Bloomsbury Group. In 1919 the Woolfs moved into Monk's House, a brick and flint building near the church, and it was from there that Virginia, suffering a mental illness in 1941, went down to the River Ouse and committed suicide. Monk's House is now owned by the National Trust.

Cross the drive, go through a gate into a rolling meadow and turn left. Over the brow of the hill descend steeply alongside a fence into the valley of Cricketing Bottom. At the foot of the slope turn left, and, in another 100 yards come to a farm road, or track.

Accommodation: For accommodation in Telscombe (youth hostel and B&B), turn right and walk between farm buildings, then continue southwest for another ½ mile or so. The track swings left through a gate and curves uphill to a narrow lane. Keep ahead along the lane into Telscombe. The youth hostel stands next to the church.

Turn left along the farm track for a little over ½ mile. When it curves left, break away to the right on a bridleway alongside a wooden fence. You then climb a short slope and cross a meadow to a road junction. Go half-left ahead and, shortly after, turn left on the road which leads down into Southease. This soon brings you to the village green by the church (grid ref: 424053). For accommodation or refreshments at the South Downs youth hostel, see Stage 11.

Southease consists of a few 17th-century cottages, a village green and an attractive church with a rare circular tower built in the 12th century, and some faded medieval wall paintings. Southease was first recorded in a charter of AD 966 granting the church and manor – and that of nearby Telscombe – to Hyde Abbey in Winchester. The village was then known as 'Sueise' and the charter, made by the Anglo-Saxon King Edgar (Eadgar), included 28 hides of land. In the Domesday Book of 1086 the village rated 27 hides and 'the villeins are assessed for 38,500 herrings and at £4 for porpoises.' This reference to herrings and porpoises provides an indication of the importance of the village as a fishery. At the time the River Ouse was a major tidal river, and it is thought possible that the lake in the grounds of Southease Place may once have been a harbour.

Southease church has a rare circular tower built in the 12th century

STAGE 11

Southease to Alfriston

Distance	7 miles (11km)
Maps	Harvey South Downs Way 1:40,000; OS Landranger 198 Brighton & Lewes and 199 Eastbourne & Hastings 1:50,000; OS Explorer 122 South Downs Way, Steyning to Newhaven and 123 South Downs Way, Newhaven to Eastbourne 1:25,000
Accommodation	Southease, Firle (+1¼ miles), Alciston (+1 mile), Alfriston
Refreshments	Southease

See map on page 42

After crossing the River Ouse the Way climbs onto the back of the Downs at Itford Hill, then proceeds for mile on mile over cropped grass with breezy open spaces and a sense that the end of the journey is drawing near, now that the Downs are curving towards the coast. On Beddingham Hill a pair of tall radio masts intrude upon the open aspect of the way, but thereafter there's little to disturb the views. Ancient burial mounds punctuate the route all along this stage, but on Bostal Hill it's multi-coloured paragliders that capture your attention at weekends and holidays, when conditions allow.

Beyond the village green in Southease, the road continues across the Ouse Valley, flanked by reedy drainage ditches, with Itford Hill seen rising ahead. Cross the bridge over the River Ouse and continue to Southease Station and a level crossing (caution!). Approaching Itford Farm bear right and walk alongside a wall to a footbridge which crosses the A26. (This goes behind South Downs YHA hostel (accommodation; refreshments for non-residents in the Courtyard Café).) On the

163

far side the SDW joins a track winding up the slope of Itford Hill, gaining views to Newhaven down the valley. Making a loop over grass slopes adorned with cowslips in spring, you come onto the crown of Itford Hill where Red Lion Pond allows a fine view to Lewes and the gap cut through the inner Downs by the River Ouse.

From here continue north-east to Beddingham Hill. Shortly before reaching the radio masts you join a clear track that takes you along the left-hand side of the masts and on across the Downs, now heading east. When the track makes a sharp curve to the right, leave it and go ahead through a gate and across a large meadow to the head of a narrow road and a car park (grid ref: 468059).

Accommodation: By descending along the road, the small village of **Firle** may be reached by those who have booked accommodation there.

Firle, or West Firle, as the Ordnance Survey shows it, is a compact village nestling at the foot of the Downs. The elegant Firle Place, which stands in parkland near the church and is backed by woodland, was originally built for the Gage family in 1557, but then rebuilt nearly 200 years later – the Georgian outer retaining the early Tudor core. East of Firle Place stands the round folly of Firle Tower (a private house), which can be seen from the Downs near Firle Beacon, and east again from that is Charleston Farmhouse. For several decades this was home to the somewhat unconventional Bloomsbury Group of writers and painters, after having been discovered by Leonard and Virginia Woolf in 1916. The house, which is open to the public, now contains works by Virginia's sister, Vanessa Bell, and Duncan Grant who died in 1978 at the age of 93.

Through the car park the SDW continues past ancient burial mounds to Firle Beacon, whose trig point stands just to the left of the trail (grid ref: 485059). A very fine panorama is gained from the scarp edge here, including Seaford Head and the start of the Seven Sisters beyond the estuary of Cuckmere Haven. Now the Way curves south-eastward and, before reaching Bostal Hill, it descends to a saddle at the head of another narrow road.

Accommodation: Descent along this road leads to a path which goes to Alciston, and is useful for those who have booked accommodation there.

Paragliders, like giant butterflies, are launched from Bostal Hill

Pass along the right-hand side of the car park on a flinty track that takes you over Bostal Hill, which claims yet another huge panoramic view, this one taking in Arlington Reservoir to the north-east.

Over the hill the track gives way to a grass trail leading on across the Downs. After a meadow section go through a gate and maintain direction along the side of a large field. As Alfriston comes into view below, Cuckmere Haven can also be seen to the south.

At the bottom of the field there's a multi-junction of tracks at Long Burgh (a long barrow not shown on the 1:50,000 map). Go ahead briefly on a narrow bridleway between scrub, then on a continuing chalk track – a drove road formerly used by shepherds to take their flocks to market. Remain with this track all the way down to King's Ride, a residential street on the edge of

Alfriston. On coming to a minor crossroads maintain direction to reach Alfriston High Street next to The Star Inn at grid ref: 520031.

Alfriston (accommodation, refreshments) is very much a show-piece village with many interesting and picturesque buildings, several of which have typical downland flint walls. The timber-framed George Inn (built 1397) is said to have been a smuggler's haunt, while The Star Inn opposite, which dates from the 15th century, bears the figurehead of a Dutch ship that foundered in Cuckmere Haven in 1672. The 14th-century church of St Andrew, standing between the greensward of The Tye and the Cuckmere River, is often referred to as 'the Cathedral of the Downs' on account of its size. Nearby the thatched, half-timbered Clergy House is of similar age to the church, and was the first building bought (in 1896) by the National Trust – for just £10! Alfriston has several shops, a post office, restaurants, pubs and tearooms, and a choice of accommodation. There are bus services to Berwick (connecting trains to Lewes/London and Eastbourne), Hailsham, Seaford, and Eastbourne.

STAGE 12

Alfriston to Eastbourne
(Footpath route via the Seven Sisters)

Distance	10½ miles (17km)
Maps	Harvey South Downs Way 1:40,000; OS Landranger 199 Eastbourne & Hastings 1:50,000; OS Explorer 123 South Downs Way, Newhaven to Eastbourne 1:25,000
Accommodation	Westdean, Exceat, Foxhole (& camping), Birling Gap, Eastbourne
Refreshments	Litlington, Exceat, Birling Gap, Beachy Head, Eastbourne

See map on page 27

Two options exist for the final stage to Eastbourne. This, the footpath option, is the recommended route for walkers, but the alternative bridleway route via Jevington (described as Stage 12a) also makes a splendid day's walk. Given the opportunity, it would be well worth tackling both!

The route via the Seven Sisters is without question the most diverse and scenically spectacular stage since leaving Winchester. It begins alongside the meandering Cuckmere River as far as Litlington, then takes a hilly path away from the river, briefly visits Westdean, then climbs over a forested spur of the Downs before descending to Exceat and the A259. From Exceat the Way enters the Seven Sisters Country Park and heads towards Cuckmere Haven, mostly avoiding a busy riverside path, before climbing to Haven Brow and the roller-coaster clifftop trail along the dramatic Seven Sisters, and over Beachy Head as a prelude to the final steep descent to Eastbourne – a worthy finish to this long walk.

Facing The George Inn turn left along Alfriston High Street as far as the Market Cross where the road forks. Turn right into River Lane (a small side street), at the bottom of which

167

Alfriston's church is known as the 'Cathedral of the Downs'

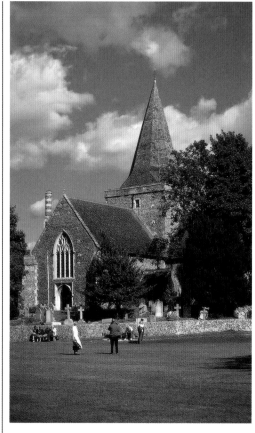

Litlington is a picturesque village of flint-faced cottages and a small Norman church with a white weatherboarded bell-tower and a shingled cap. Tucked under the Downs on the east bank of the Cuckmere, it is said that smugglers once had an underground passageway leading from the old Rectory to other houses within the village.

you bear right again alongside the Cuckmere River, with the church now ahead. Cross the bridleway bridge with its white railings, and immediately turn right onto a riverside path. The walker's route has now departed from that of the bridleway for the last time.

There now follows a pleasant riverside walk of about a mile as far as **Litlington** ◄ (accommodation, refreshments), where the path forks.

The **Vanguard Way** is a recreational long distance route which journeys from East Croydon railway station to Seaford Head and Newhaven. Devised by The Vanguards Rambling Club, the original route was 62 miles (100km) long, but a more recent extension to Newhaven has added another 4 miles to it. See *The Vanguard Way* by Colin Saunders (available from RA National Office).

Accommodation: For Alfriston Youth Hostel continue ahead for a few paces, then cross the river by footbridge.

Bear left into the village where you emerge near The Plough and Harrow pub, then right along the road until it bends to the right. Branch left here, then go through a kissing gate and up the slope ahead, from where you have a fine view across the valley to a white horse carved in the slopes of High and Over.

The Way now edges fields and shares the route of the **Vanguard Way** before descending towards Friston Forest in Charleston Bottom. Passing behind **Charleston Manor**, a series of steps then takes you up into the mainly broad-leaved **Friston Forest**. ▶ At the top of the incline you come onto a track which takes you through the forest heading first south, then south-west where you make the descent to the attractive hamlet of **Westdean**.

Friston Forest covers almost 2000 acres of mainly broad-leaved woodland. Owned by South East Water, but managed by the Forestry Commission, the forest was planted as a means of protecting underground water sources from pollution.

Charleston Manor is an historic building mentioned in the Domesday Book as being owned by William the Conqueror's cup-bearer, Cerlestone. In the grounds the restored tithe barn is 177 feet (54m) long, with a massive tiled roof and a medieval circular dovecote. The gardens are open to the public on set days in the summer.

Westdean is a very small village tucked within a fold of the Downs almost encircled by Friston Forest. It is thought that Alfred the Great built a palace here in AD 850, although no trace has been found. However, there is a 13th-century flint-built rectory and a part-Norman church nearby.

The Way crosses high meadows above Litlington, the Cuckmere Valley below

Exceat was once a flourishing village, until the Black Death virtually wiped it from the map in the 15th century.

On coming to a road, walk ahead a short distance to a junction opposite a duck pond. Next to the pond a track leads to another flight of steps – more than 200 of them! – that climb once more into Friston Forest. At the top of the steps a footpath continues to a low wall with a built-in stone stile, an information board and a splendid view over the snaking course of the Cuckmere steeply below. This is a charming spot from which to survey the Cuckmere Valley, its water meadows, and the green wave of the Downs beyond, reaching towards the Channel.

You now descend a steep meadow to **Exceat** ◀ (accommodation, refreshments) and the A259 near the **Seven Sisters Country Park Visitor Centre** (grid ref: 519995). There's a bus stop nearby for buses travelling to Eastbourne.

The **Seven Sisters Country Park** covers an area of 690 acres on the east side of the Cuckmere River south of Exceat. Established in 1971 by East Sussex County Council, but managed by the Sussex Downs Conservation Board, the visitor centre is housed in a converted 18th-century barn at Exceat. It has an interesting wildlife and local history exhibition, a gift shop and toilets, with a convenient restaurant next door – which also offers B&B.

Cross the road with care and go through a gate with a concrete farm drive stretching ahead, but leave it at once to go left, then immediately right where SDW signs direct you across a rising slope of cropped downland. On reaching the highest part of the slope there's a stone marker to indicate the site where Exceat's 11th-century church once stood. With little evidence of a path on the ground, low waymark posts now lead you down to a kissing gate and a concrete farm road.

Cross the road and walk ahead on a broad path with the Cuckmere River to the right, and moments later veer left to take the SDW trail rising alongside a fence. This takes you onto the clifftop of Haven Brow with lovely views of **Cuckmere Haven** and Seaford Head on the far side. The Way now turns south-east on a switchback route across the Seven Sisters, with the sea stretching away to the right and charming green country rolling into the distance. It's an energetic stretch, with steep descents between the 'Sisters' into dry valleys or 'bottoms', followed by steep ascents that will test your level of fitness after several days of walking.

Cuckmere Haven is the estuary of the Cuckmere River, a shingle bank protected by the cliffs of Haven Brow and Seaford Head. In the 15th century it was more open than it is today, for in 1460 French raiders sailed up the river to Exceat and attacked the village. During the 18th century the Haven was a notorious landing place for smugglers, when contraband goods would be brought upstream to Exceat and Alfriston. As recently as 1923 smugglers were caught there with a haul of expensive brandy. A little inland from the Haven itself an artificial lagoon attracts assorted waders, while the snaking Cuckmere between Exceat and the Haven is busy with swans, tufted ducks, dabchicks, cormorants and herons.

Beyond Haven Brow there's Short Brow, then Rough Brow, and Flagstaff Brow with its dedication stone, and Flat Hill, Baily's Hill and, finally, Michel Dean on which an obelisk records the dedication of this land to the National Trust in memory of two brothers killed in the First World War.

You then slope down to Birling Gap (accommodation, refreshments), a surprisingly drab place in the midst of such beautiful scenery, it consists of a car park, small hotel, café, toilet block, telephone kiosk, coastguard's office, and a few 19th-century cottages (built to house coastguards' families) precariously situated on the crumbling cliffs. The National Trust purchased Birling Gap as part of its Enterprise Neptune scheme aimed at protecting large sections of coastline, but it is being steadily eroded by the remorseless action of the tides.

Beachy Head, some 536 feet (163m) above the waves, is one of the best-known features of the Sussex coast. The famous red and white ringed lighthouse at its base was erected in 1902, with both the builders and the stone from which it was built, being lowered from the clifftop by cableway.

Pass to the left of the coastguard's building, then bear half-right up a slope of scrub to reach the former **lighthouse of Belle Tout**, a stumpy building that has been converted into a private house and luxury B&B with tremendous views in all directions (www.belletoute.co.uk). Go round the inland side of the boundary wall and down the drive beyond towards a road, then up a short slope before dropping into Shooter's Bottom. The Way then climbs to **Beachy Head**, ◄ virtually the last ascent of the long walk, with dramatic views to enjoy of the lighthouse steeply below. Beware not to stray too close to the edge, for early in 1999 a massive rockfall destroyed a section of the cliff-face, and it's none too stable. For refreshments go down to the road where you'll find the Beachy Head Inn and visitor centre.

Belle Tout lighthouse predates that below Beachy Head by 70 years. Built in 1832 of Aberdeen granite by 'Mad Jack' Fuller, the eccentric squire of Brightling, it served as the lighthouse for this stretch of coast until 1902, but was replaced because the light would often be lost in fog. It has now been converted to a private dwelling, and following a major cliff-fall from Beachy Head in 1999, it was physically moved a short distance away from the cliff edge.

The continuing route skirts the cliff edge and becomes a tarmac path leading round to a spur from which you gain a splendid view back to Beachy Head lighthouse. Beyond this vantage point a marker post directs the SDW to veer right along the seaward flank of the slope above Whitebread Hole (a sports field can be seen below) with Eastbourne in view ahead. On the northern side of Whitebread Hole, go up a little to

*Beachy Head
lighthouse*

another marker post where you curve right and descend a final steep grass slope to the official end of the walk, marked by a notice board beside a small café on Dukes Drive (grid ref: 600972).

Congratulations on completing this very fine walk. I hope you enjoyed it as much as I did.

Extended Route: Although Dukes Drive marks the official end of the South Downs Way, you may find that a more satisfactory conclusion would be

173

Eastbourne Pier, another 1½ miles on. To reach this simply walk ahead along Dukes Drive to King Edward's Parade. You can follow this to the Grand Parade which leads directly to the pier, or vary the walk by going through the adjacent gardens on the right. Eastbourne Pier is at grid ref: 617989, and the railway station is easily reached from there.

Eastbourne, with its flower beds and bowling greens, has retained an air of gentility and become a perennial favourite with retired folk. The original settlement of East Bourne had a church before the Norman invasion. There were neighbouring hamlets called South Bourne and Sea Houses, the latter a collection of fishermen's cottages, but the three were amalgamated in the mid 19th century and in 1910 Eastbourne was created a borough. Along the front, north of the pier, stands The Redoubt, a sturdy, circular building – mostly of brick – erected in the early 1800s as part of the coastal defence system against feared invasion by Napoleon. The martello tower known as the Wish Tower, south-west of the pier, also formed part of those defences.

STAGE 12(a)

Alfriston to Eastbourne
(Bridleway route inland via Jevington)

Distance	8 miles (12½km)
Maps	Harvey South Downs Way 1:40,000; OS Landranger 199 Eastbourne & Hastings 1:50,000; OS Explorer 123 South Downs Way, Newhaven to Eastbourne 1:25,000
Accommodation	Milton Street (+¾ mile), Wilmington (+1 mile), Jevington, Eastbourne
Refreshments	Jevington and Eastbourne

See map on page 34

This bridleway alternative to the Seven Sisters route is no second best, and walkers as well as cyclists and horse-riders should enjoy the constant variety of the folding Downs and exquisite views that are revealed shortly after setting out. It does not take long to escape Alfriston, with the steady ascent of Windover Hill reaching a point above the unseen head of England's largest chalk figure, the Long Man of Wilmington. Up there one has a tremendous sense of space as you gaze across the Cuckmere's valley to the line of the South Downs, along which the previous stage journeyed. Ahead the Downs are broad-backed and seemingly endless, although it's a relatively short distance to travel before you descend to Jevington in its streamless valley. South-east of this final village on the South Downs Way, a bridleway ascends Bourne Hill and then coincides with the Wealdway across Foxhole Brow and Beachy Brow alongside a golf course with Eastbourne seen below. The route continues south of the A259 and, soon after crossing the B2103, with the coast in sight, it swoops down a grass slope to end alongside the footpath route on the edge of Eastbourne at Duke's Drive.

Wilmington, seen from Wilmington Hill above the Long Man's head

Emerging in Alfriston beside The Star Inn turn left along the High Street as far as the Market Cross where the road forks. Here you turn right into River Lane (a small side street), and right again alongside the Cuckmere River. Shortly after bear left and cross a bridleway bridge, on the east side of which you part company with the footpath route which takes the riverside path heading downstream.

Keep ahead on the tarmac path, and immediately after crossing a small side stream bear left through a small patch of woodland, then continue through a water meadow to a bridle gate which gives out to a minor road junction. Cross ahead, then take a bridleway on the right which becomes a delightful sunken track overhung mostly with ash trees.

Accommodation: If you've arranged accommodation in Milton Street, do not go up this track, but take the minor road ahead.

The track comes onto a very narrow lane by a small car park.

Accommodation: For   accommodation   and/or refreshments in Wilmington, turn left along this lane.

Cross directly ahead where the track, a one-time coach road, winds up onto Windover Hill where various mounds and depressions betray the site of burial barrows and the refuse pits from neolithic flint mines. As you gain height, so the views to the right become more expansive, but an even better panorama may be gained from the top of the hill when you reach a field gate with a bridle gate next to it. Before going through the bridle gate, stray left for a moment onto the lip of the escarpment, for the view from this point is one of the best of the whole route. Immediately below, on the scarp slope facing north, is the **Long Man of Wilmington**, although he cannot be seen from here.

The Long Man of Wilmington is England's largest chalk figure, standing 226 feet (69m) high, with outstretched arms and a stave held in each hand. Although his presence was first recorded in 1779, no-one knows his true origin. One theory suggests that he dates from the Bronze Age, another that the Long Man is an Iron Age fertility symbol, yet another says he represents the Saxon King Harold. We do know that in 1874 the outline of the figure was re-cut, but this was reinforced in 1969 by more than 700 concrete blocks to protect the exposed chalk and make it more visible. The Long Man is in the care of the Sussex Archaeological Trust.

Wilmington village is the nearest cluster of buildings to the north, and beyond that, Arlington Reservoir focuses the Wealden view which extends to the distant blue line of Ashdown Forest. To the west, across the Cuckmere's valley, the downland wall should be familiar from your recent travels across Firle Beacon and Bostal Hill.

Wilmington is an old village going back to Saxon times. Attractively set at the foot of the Downs, the main street is lined with charming cottages and overhung with trees. The flint-walled church has a 12th-century chancel, and next door the remains of a Benedictine priory founded in 1100. There's also a Tudor house by the priory containing a fascinating agricultural museum, and in the churchyard a huge yew tree thought to be up to 1600 years old, its ancient limbs supported by wooden props and chains.

Go through the bridle gate and take the right-hand track alongside a wire fence above the coombe of Deep Dean. Very soon the Way veers away from the fence and curves uphill a little, guided by marker posts. Then, after a lengthy stretch of open downland, you go through another bridle gate and curve slightly left towards a hedge-line where you'll find yet another gate. The bridleway then goes ahead to a crossing track, where you turn left to slope downhill through woodland.

When the way forks take the right branch and keep ahead at a crossing track with the first buildings of Jevington coming into view. Arriving by the parish church remain on the driveway which leads to **Jevington**'s (accommodation, refreshments) main street opposite the Hungry Monk Restaurant. (For refreshments at the Eight Bells pub, turn left.)

Jevington was once the haunt of smugglers bringing their bounty inland from Birling Gap below Beachy Head. The parish church of St Andrew has an impressive Saxon tower and a bell said to have been brought ashore from a shipwreck. The main village street has some attractive flint-walled houses and a popular pub, The Eight Bells, that was once owned by smuggler, James Pettit, known as 'Jevington Jigg' who was eventually sentenced to serve 17 years in Botany Bay.

Turn right, then left by Jevington Tea Gardens on a minor lane that soon becomes another track rising up the slopes of Bourne Hill (not shown as such on the 1:50,000 map). At the head of the slope you arrive at a junction of tracks (grid ref: 577009) to be joined briefly by the **Wealdway**. Note the nearby stone marker which mentions Old Town Eastbourne and Jevington. Apparently it was brought here from the old Barclays Bank building in Eastbourne, which was bombed during the Second World War.

The **Wealdway** is a long-distance recreational route of 82 miles (132km), which links the River Thames at Gravesend in Kent, with the English Channel at Beachy Head. On the way it crosses the North Downs, several High Wealden ridges, Ashdown Forest, and finally, the South Downs.

Continue straight ahead and you'll soon gain a first view of Eastbourne. About ¾ mile from the Wealdway junction pass a dew pond on your left, and a little later as you come to a golf course, note a signpost directing a path (used by the Wealdway) to the left, which goes to Eastbourne Youth Hostel. Unless you plan to spend the night there, continue ahead to reach the A259.

Cross with care onto a brief stony section which soon becomes a grass trail striking ahead (aiming southeast). About 50 yards before reaching a trig point there's a bridleway junction. Ignore that which slants off to the left and keep ahead to pass the trig point and a dew pond on your left. The way curves to the right, and shortly after, at another signed junction, you veer slightly left down the slope, then follow along the edge of trees as far as a road junction. Cross the B2103 (**caution!**) to the left of this junction, and continue over more open downland a little below the crestline.

On coming to a signed 4-way crossing, turn sharp left and go down the slope with views ahead of Eastbourne and a long stretch of coastline. The way

Old marker stone on Bourne Hill above Jevington

steepens towards the foot of the slope where it is funnelled through a grassy gully, then swings to the right just above a road, soon reaching the end of the South Downs Way beside a small café on Duke's Drive.

Congratulations on completing the South Downs Way!

For information about Eastbourne, please refer to details given at the end of the footpath route description under Stage 12 above.

APPENDIX A
Useful Addresses

The Long Distance Walkers Association
www.ldwa.org.uk

The Ramblers
2nd Floor, Camelford House
87–90 Albert Embankment
London
SE1 7TW
Tel: 020 7339 8500
www.ramblers.org.uk

Youth Hostels Association
(England & Wales)
Trevelyan House
Dimple Road
Matlock
DE4 3YH
Tel: 01629 592 700
www.yha.org.uk

South Downs Way Officer
South Downs Way Team
South Downs National Park Authority
Stanmer Park Offices
Stanmer Park
Lewes Road
Brighton
BN1 9SE
Tel: 01273 625242
www.nationaltrail.co.uk/
south-downs-way
www.southdowns.gov.uk

The South Downs Society
2 Swan Court
Station Road
Pulborough
RH20 1RL
Tel: 01798 875073
www.southdownssociety.org.uk

The South Downs online
www.southdowns.gov.uk

Tourist Information Centres
Arundel TIC
1–3 Crown Yard Mews
River Road
Arundel
BN18 9JW
Tel: 01903 882268
www.sussexbythesea.com

Eastbourne TIC
Cornfield Road
Eastbourne
BN21 4QA
Tel: 0871 663 0031
tic@eastbourne.gov.uk

Lewes TIC
187 High Street
Lewes
BN7 2DE
Tel: 01273 483448
lewes.tic@lewes.gov.uk
www.enjoysussex.info

Petersfield TIC
The Library
27 The Square
Petersfield
GU32 3HH
Tel: 01730 268829
www.easthants.gov.uk/tourism

Winchester TIC
The Guildhall
The Broadway
Winchester
SO23 9GH
Tel: 01962 840500
www.visitwinchester.co.uk

APPENDIX B
Public Transport Information

Rail travel
For information in regard to rail travel, timetables and fares, contact
National Rail Enquiries
Tel: 0845 748 4950
www.nationalrail.co.uk

Bookings can be made online at
www.qjump.co.uk or
www.thetrainline.com.

Bus travel
Traveline
Tel: 0871 200 2233 (10p/min +)
www.traveline.org.uk

National Express
0870 580 8080

APPENDIX C

Recommended Reading

	Illustrated Guide to Britain (AA/Drive Publications)
Armstrong, R.	*A History of Sussex* (Phillimore)
Baker, M.	*Sussex Villages* (Robert Hale)
Brandon, P.	*The South Saxons* (Phillimore)
	The Sussex Landscape (Hodder & Stoughton)
	Sussex (Making of the English Landscape series, Hodder & Stoughton)
Darby, B.	*South Downs* (Robert Hale)
	View of Sussex (Robert Hale)
Dillon, P.	*The National Trails* (Cicerone Press)
Edwards, P.	*Mountain Biking on the South Downs* (Cicerone Press)
Godfrey, J.	*Sussex* (New Shell Guides series, Michael Joseph)
Harrison, D.	*Along the South Downs Way* (Cassell)
Hillier, C. and Mosley, J.	*Images of the Downs* (McMillan)
Hudson, W. H.	*Nature in Downland* (London)
Jebb, M.	*A Guide to the South Downs Way* (Constable)
Jefferies, R.	*Nature Near London* (John Clare Books)
Mason, O.	*South-East England* (Bartholomew)
Millmore, P.	*South Downs Way* (Aurum Press)
Moore, C.	*Green Roof of Sussex* (Middleton Press)
O'Dell, N.	*Portrait of Hampshire* (Robert Hale)
Perkins, B.	*South Downs Way for Motorists* (Frederick Warne)
Pyatt, E. C.	*Chalkways of South and South-East England* (David & Charles)
Reynolds, K.	*Walking in Sussex* (Cicerone Press)
	Walks in the South Downs National Park (Cicerone Press)
	Classic Walks in Southern England (Oxford Illustrated Press)
Sankey, J.	*Nature Guide to South-East England* (Usborne)
Scholes, R.	*Understanding the Countryside* (Moorland Publishing)
Spence, K.	*The Companion Guide to Kent & Sussex* (Collins)
White, J. T.	*The South-East, Down and Weald* (Eyre-Methuen)
Woodford, C.	*Portrait of Sussex* (Robert Hale)

183

APPENDIX D
Stage by Stage Westwards

STAGE 1
Eastbourne to Alfriston (Footpath route via the Seven Sisters)
Distance: 10½ miles (17km)
Passes through Eastbourne, Birling Gap, Westdean, Litlington and Alfriston

STAGE 1(a)
Eastbourne to Alfriston (Bridleway route inland via Jevington)
Distance: 8 miles (12½km)
Passes through Eastbourne, Jevington and Alfriston

STAGE 2
Alfriston to Southease
Distance: 7 miles (11km)
Passes through Alfriston and Southease, option takes in Rodmell

STAGE 3
Southease to Housedean (A27)
Distance: 6 miles (9½km)
Passes through Southease

STAGE 4
Housedean (A27) to Pyecombe
Distance: 8½ miles (13½km)
Passes through Pyecombe

STAGE 5
Pyecombe to Botolphs (Adur Valley)
Distance: 7½ miles (12km)
Passes Pyecombe and Saddlescombe

STAGE 6
Botolphs to Washington
Distance: 7 miles (11km)
Passes through Botolphs

STAGE 7
Washington to Amberley
Distance: 6 miles (9½km)
Passes through no towns or villages on route, but alternative passes through Washington, and ends on edge of Amberley.

STAGE 8
Amberley to Cocking
Distance: 12 miles (19km)
Passes through no towns or villages on route but arrives close to Cocking

STAGE 9
Cocking to South Harting
Distance: 7½ miles (12km)
Passe through no towns or villages on route but comes close to South Hasting

STAGE 10
South Harting to Buriton (Queen Elizabeth Forest)
Distance: 3½ miles (5½km)
Passes through no towns or villages on route but Buriton is nearby

STAGE 11
Buriton to Exton
Distance: 12 miles (19km)
Passes through Queen Elizabeth Country Park, Mercury Park and Exton. Bridleway passes though Warnford but avoids Exton

STAGE 12
Exton to Winchester
Distance: 12 miles (19km)
Passes through Exton and Winchester

APPENDIX E
Stage by Stage Eastwards

STAGE 1
Winchester to Exton
Distance: 12 miles (19km)
Passes through Winchester and Exton

STAGE 2
Exton to Buriton
Distance: 12 miles (19km)
Passes through Exton, Mercury Park and Queen Elizabeth Country Park
Bridleway passes though Warnford but avoids Exton

STAGE 3
Buriton (Queen Elizabeth Forest) to South Harting
Distance: 3½ miles (5½km)
Passes through no towns or villages on route but South Harting is nearby

STAGE 4
South Harting to Cocking
Distance: 7½ miles (12km)
Passe through no towns or villages on route but comes close to Cocking

STAGE 5
Cocking to Amberley
Distance: 12 miles (19km)
Passes through no towns or villages on route but arrives on edge of Amberley

STAGE 6
Amberley to Washington
Distance: 6 miles (9½km)
Passes through no towns or villages on route

STAGE 7
Washington to Botolphs
Distance: 7 miles (11km)
Passes through Botolphs

STAGE 8
Botolphs (Adur Valley) to Pyecombe
Distance: 7½ miles (12km)
Passes Saddlescombe and Pyecombe

STAGE 9
Pyecombe to Housedean (A27)
Distance: 8½ miles (13½km)
Passes through Pyecombe

STAGE 10
Housedean (A27) to Southease
Distance: 6 miles (9½km)
Passes through Southease

STAGE 11
Southease to Alfriston
Distance: 7 miles (11km)
Passes through Southease and Alfriston, option takes in Rodmell

STAGE 12
Alfriston to Eastbourne (Footpath route via the Seven Sisters)
Distance: 10½ miles (17km)
Passes through Alfriston, Litlington, Westdean, Birling Gap, and Eastbourne

STAGE 12 (a)
Alfriston to Eastbourne (Bridleway route inland via Jevington)
Distance: 8 miles (12½km)
Passes through Alfriston, Jevington and Eastbourne

LISTING OF CICERONE GUIDES

Walking in the Auvergne
Walking in the Cevennes
Walking in the Dordogne
Walking in the Haute Savoie –
  North & South
Walking in the Languedoc
Walking in the Tarentaise and
  Beaufortain Alps
Walks in the Cathar Region

GERMANY
Germany's Romantic Road
Hiking and Biking in the
  Black Forest
Walking in the Bavarian Alps

HIMALAYA
Annapurna
Bhutan
Everest
Garhwal and Kumaon
Langtang with Gosainkund
  and Helambu
Manaslu
The Mount Kailash Trek
Trekking in Ladakh
Trekking in the Himalaya

ICELAND & GREENLAND
Trekking in Greenland
Walking and Trekking in Iceland

IRELAND
Irish Coastal Walks
The Irish Coast to Coast Walk
The Mountains of Ireland

ITALY
Gran Paradiso
Sibillini National Park
Shorter Walks in the Dolomites
Through the Italian Alps
Trekking in the Apennines
Trekking in the Dolomites
Via Ferratas of the Italian
  Dolomites: Vols 1 & 2
Walking in Abruzzo
Walking in Italy's Stelvio
  National Park
Walking in Sardinia
Walking in Sicily
Walking in the Central
  Italian Alps
Walking in the Dolomites
Walking in Tuscany
Walking in Umbria

Walking on the Amalfi Coast
Walking the Italian Lakes

MEDITERRANEAN
Jordan – Walks, Treks, Caves,
  Climbs and Canyons
The Ala Dag
The High Mountains of Crete
The Mountains of Greece
Treks and Climbs in Wadi Rum
Walking in Malta
Western Crete

NORTH AMERICA
British Columbia
The Grand Canyon
The John Muir Trail
The Pacific Crest Trail

SOUTH AMERICA
Aconcagua and the
  Southern Andes
Hiking and Biking Peru's
  Inca Trails
Torres del Paine

SCANDINAVIA
Walking in Norway

SLOVENIA, CROATIA AND
MONTENEGRO
The Islands of Croatia
The Julian Alps of Slovenia
The Mountains of Montenegro
Trekking in Slovenia
Walking in Croatia
Walking in Slovenia: The
  Karavanke

SPAIN AND PORTUGAL
Costa Blanca: West
Mountain Walking in
  Southern Catalunya
The Mountains of Central Spain
The Mountains of Nerja
The Northern Caminos
Trekking through Mallorca
Walking in Madeira
Walking in Mallorca
Walking in Menorca
Walking in the Algarve
Walking in the Cordillera
  Cantabrica
Walking in the Sierra Nevada
Walking on Gran Canaria

Walking on La Gomera and
  El Hierro
Walking on La Palma
Walking on Lanzarote and
  Fuerteventura
Walking on Tenerife
Walking the GR7 in Andalucia
Walks and Climbs in the
  Picos de Europa

SWITZERLAND
Alpine Pass Route
Central Switzerland
The Bernese Alps
The Swiss Alps
Tour of the Jungfrau Region
Walking in the Valais
Walking in Ticino
Walks in the Engadine

TECHNIQUES
Geocaching in the UK
Indoor Climbing
Lightweight Camping
Map and Compass
Mountain Weather
Moveable Feasts
Outdoor Photography
Polar Exploration
Rock Climbing
Sport Climbing
The Book of the Bivvy
The Hillwalker's Guide to
  Mountaineering
The Hillwalker's Manual

MINI GUIDES
Alpine Flowers
Avalanche!
Navigating with a GPS
Navigation
Pocket First Aid and
  Wilderness Medicine
Snow

MOUNTAIN LITERATURE
8000 metres
A Walk in the Clouds
Unjustifiable Risk?

For full information on all our
guides, books and eBooks,
visit our website:
www.cicerone.co.uk.

Walking – Trekking – Mountaineering – Climbing – Cycling

Over 40 years, Cicerone have built up an outstanding collection of 300 guides, inspiring all sorts of amazing adventures.

Every guide comes from extensive exploration and research by our expert authors, all with a passion for their subjects. They are frequently praised, endorsed and used by clubs, instructors and outdoor organisations.

All our titles can now be bought as **e-books** and many as iPad and Kindle files and we will continue to make all our guides available for these and many other devices.

Our website shows any **new information** we've received since a book was published. Please do let us know if you find anything has changed, so that we can pass on the latest details. On our **website** you'll also find some great ideas and lots of information, including sample chapters, contents lists, reviews, articles and a photo gallery.

It's easy to keep in touch with what's going on at Cicerone, by getting our monthly **free e-newsletter**, which is full of offers, competitions, up-to-date information and topical articles. You can subscribe on our home page and also follow us on **Facebook** and **Twitter**, as well as our **blog**.

Cicerone – the very best guides for exploring the world.

ℭ𝔦ℭℰ𝔯𝔒𝔫ℰ

2 Police Square Milnthorpe Cumbria LA7 7PY
Tel: 015395 62069 info@cicerone.co.uk
www.cicerone.co.uk